THE OTHER SIDE

STORIES FROM THE AFTERLIFE

BEYOND
THE FRAY PUBLISHING
SINCE 2015

ISBN 13: 979-8-89234-132-5

Cover design: L. Douglas Hogan

Beyond The Fray Publishing
A division of Beyond The Fray, LLC
San Diego, CA
www.beyondthefraypublishing.com

BEYOND
THE FRAY PUBLISHING
SINCE 2019

CONTENTS

INTRODUCTION

What happens when we die? It's a question as old as humanity itself—one that transcends cultures, religions, and philosophies. Despite the countless theories, beliefs, and scientific explanations, the mystery of what lies beyond our final breath remains one of life's greatest enigmas. Yet, there are those who claim to have glimpsed the other side.

The Other Side: Stories From the Afterlife is a collection of fourteen firsthand accounts from individuals who have crossed the threshold of death and returned to tell their stories. These are not secondhand tales or distant legends, but vivid, deeply personal experiences recounted by the very people who lived them—or, perhaps more accurately, died them. Each narrative offers a unique window into the afterlife, revealing encounters with brilliant light, overwhelming peace, shadowy realms, and profound revelations that defy earthly understanding.

These stories are as diverse as the people who tell them. Some describe transcendent beauty and unconditional love, while others recount unsettling journeys through dark, unfamiliar landscapes. Regardless of the details, each account shares a common thread: the experience was real, transformative, and impossible to forget.

This book does not seek to prove or disprove what happens after death. Instead, it invites you to listen with an open mind and heart. These are stories of hope, fear, wonder, and the enduring mystery of existence itself. Whether you're a skeptic, a believer, or simply curious, *The Other Side* challenges you to consider the possibility that death may not be the end, but rather the beginning of something we have yet to fully understand.

ONE
AMBER CAVANAUGH

SHE DIED DURING A STROKE AND WAS SHOWN THE PURPOSE OF OUR EXISTENCE

Amber Cavanaugh shares her profound experience following a stroke in 2021. She recounts the choices made during her near-death experience, emphasizing the significance of connections beyond the physical realm and embracing her purpose to positively impact others. Her journey underscores the transformative power of adversity and the constant support from the spiritual realm.

———

Amber Cavanaugh had always felt connected to other worlds. Long before her near-death experience, she lived a life that most people might label extraordinary or even surreal. From early childhood, Amber could see and communicate with spirits, sensing presences and energies that others rarely perceived. Her mother would find her, at times, engaged in hushed conversations in empty rooms. As a small girl, Amber spoke of "visitors" who brought her messages and comfort. While some parents might have brushed off such talk as a child's overactive imagination, Amber's family learned that her abilities were authentic, too vivid and consistent to discount.

As she grew older, her gifts blossomed beyond mediumship. She realized she was also a psychic, capable of glimpsing events and possibilities yet to unfold. She discovered that she had the ability to place her hands on people—or even animals—and sense the source of physical or emotional pain, a form of medical intuition. She was an empath, feeling the emotional currents of those around her as if they were her own, sometimes to a disorienting degree. She was a healer, channeling energies that brought solace and comfort. Finally, and to the delight of any pet or stray she encountered, she learned she could communicate with animals in a way that transcended simple affection. Through gentle touches and a deep intuitive link, she

2

could glean an animal's fears, pains, or even joys, and respond with a kindness that often left observers speechless.

Her upbringing wasn't defined solely by these supernatural gifts, however. Growing up in a diverse community, Amber also nourished a passion for helping others in more conventional ways. She pursued formal education in social work and became a social worker herself, applying both her training and her empathic gifts to aid people wrestling with trauma, poverty, and countless other hardships. Whether comforting someone in crisis or connecting a struggling parent to resources, Amber strove to use every tool at her disposal—both earthly and otherwise—to make a difference.

By the time she reached adulthood, Amber's life was as multifaceted as her abilities. She had a warm and bustling household, filled with her husband, children, and even some of the former foster kids they had welcomed into their home. They weren't just wards of the state; they were extended family, bonded through trials and love. Anyone who stepped through Amber's door quickly realized that she radiated compassion, humor, and a down-to-earth practicality that balanced out her extraordinary gifts.

It was this warmth and love that were on full display at Christmastime in 2021—a season Amber held dear. Her house glowed with twinkling lights and smelled of cinnamon and pine. A festive hum filled each room as they prepared for their annual holiday traditions. On Christmas Eve, her children and their extended foster siblings gathered around a table littered with frosting tubes, candies, and gingerbread pieces, building houses that soon became candy-clad masterpieces. It was a scene of holiday magic: laughter, teasing, and the exchanging of stories, reminiscent of an old-fashioned family gathering in simpler times.

On Christmas Day, Amber felt a deep sense of gratitude. As evening settled, she and her family decided to wind down by watching a beloved Christmas movie together. The living room was full—couches and armchairs draped with holiday blankets, the soft glow of the tree in the corner. Amber should have felt nothing but cozy contentment. Instead, she was struck by a sudden, searing pain in her head. It came on so abruptly that she excused herself early, her hand pressed to her temple.

She retreated to her bedroom, texting her husband for Tylenol and Advil. At first, she believed it to be an intense migraine—something she'd experienced in the past. Yet, unbeknownst to anyone in the house, the headache's real cause was a dissected artery that had led to a massive stroke. Even as her husband approached with the pain relievers, Amber slipped into unconsciousness, the headache so debilitating that she never took the medication. By the time morning light seeped through her curtains, she woke to a world irreparably altered.

Her entire right side was paralyzed—dead weight that refused every desperate mental command she gave it. A wave of confusion crashed over her. She tried to speak, but her mouth refused to form the words, managing only a meager two. Fear clutched her heart as she recognized the signs of a stroke: garbled speech, partial paralysis, confusion. Her husband, sharing her alarm, dialed 911 without hesitation.

When paramedics arrived, Amber expected immediate help. Instead, much to her horror, they misunderstood her slurred speech and vacant expression. Perhaps mistaking her for someone under the influence, they hesitated to render stroke-specific aid. Their confusion cost her precious minutes—time that was critical when addressing potential brain damage. By the time Amber reached a local hospital, the stroke had already inflicted significant damage. Doctors administered TPA, the clot-busting drug intended to reverse or reduce the stroke's effects, but it had no effect. Making matters worse, Amber experienced an allergic reaction to the Benadryl given to mitigate side effects, compounding the crisis.

In short order, the medical team realized they were out of their depth. She needed specialized care, possibly emergency brain surgery. A helicopter was summoned for an airlift to a larger, more advanced facility. Amber's family gathered around her as she was prepared for transport, each face etched with anxiety. The doctors cautioned that her chance of surviving even the flight was slim. Her husband was granted permission to accompany her, becoming her steadfast pillar in the swirling maelstrom of critical care.

As the helicopter blades thundered overhead, lifting them skyward, sunlight poured through the windows, illuminating Amber's features. She felt a surge of heat she could not explain—an intense warmth that seemed both physical and spiritual. In that exact moment, Amber understood that she was stepping to the edge of life and death. The bright light grew more potent, eclipsing everything else. Closing her eyes, she let go.

When they reopened—in some sense—Amber was no longer in the helicopter. Instead, she found herself immersed in a vision or realm so resplendent it left her breathless. She stood in a garden of unearthly beauty: lush, shimmering foliage, each leaf and blade of grass seemingly lit from within. Soft breezes carried a scent of blossoms sweeter and richer than anything on Earth. Every color was amplified, as if someone had turned the saturation dial to its highest setting. A pond of glowing water, seemingly made of liquid gold, reflected the radiance all around.

Yet, more than the scenery itself, it was the atmosphere of pure, unconditional love that overwhelmed Amber. It was like stepping into an ocean of acceptance, every doubt and earthly worry stripped away in the face of this all-encompassing warmth. She felt no pain, no tension—only profound peace, as though she'd come home after a lifetime of traveling.

To her right, scenes of other lives flickered like windows into parallel realities. She recognized these as her own incarnations, each revealing some aspect of her soul's journey across time and dimension. There, she saw glimpses of historical eras, foreign lands, and alien landscapes, all facets of her soul's immense tapestry. The sight was both awe-inspiring and strangely comforting, like reconnecting with distant relatives you'd always felt close to but never fully known.

On her left, she sensed the presence of her current life. She could feel her children, her husband, and the extended family they had built—though they were not physically in this garden, their essence was there, radiating warmth and love. It was as if she could hear them telling her it was all right to stay or to go, that they would find their way regardless.

Standing in front of her, in the heart of the garden, was a brilliant gazebo bathed in radiant light. Inside were two familiar figures: her spirit guides, Gail and Jessica. Amber had known them for years; they'd been her mentors on the astral plane, guiding her in matters of mediumship and spiritual healing. Here, though, they shimmered with a vividness she had never witnessed. Their greetings were telepathic, an effortless exchange of thoughts and emotions that transcended language.

Her guides presented her with a choice. She could remain in this divine paradise—free from suffering, safe in eternal love—or return to her physical body to continue her earthly path. They conveyed the consequences of each option without judgment. They showed her that if she went back, the road ahead would be grueling. The next eighteen months would bring immense trials, with the first six months being especially harrowing. Yet they also high-lighted the potential for remarkable impact: the ways her renewed presence on Earth could alter the course of her family's lives, the lives of clients and strangers she would one day help, and her own spiritual evolution.

For a moment, Amber considered staying. The peace in that realm was irresistible, like sinking into a warm ocean after a lifetime of standing in the cold rain. But when she turned to her left again, seeing the loving echoes of her children, husband, and foster kids, she was overcome by love for them. She recalled all the lessons she had learned as a medium and social worker: that love, in all its forms, was worth any sacrifice.

Her mind made up, Amber conveyed her decision to her guides. In an instant, the garden began to fade. The brilliant colors dissolved, replaced by something akin to a waiting room filled with luminous light. From this vantage, she watched her physical form being carried into the larger hospital, battered by a severe seizure triggered by intense brain swelling. She saw her body convulse, doctors and nurses scrambling around it. Then, in one jarring moment, she felt her consciousness snap back into the confines of that wounded body. Unbearable pain and confusion assaulted her senses, and everything went dark.

Amber woke to find herself in a hospital bed. It was still Christmas Day—morning sunshine angled through the window, ironically bright and hopeful. Her body was partially paralyzed, and forming coherent sentences felt like scaling a mountain. The stroke had ravaged her speech centers, but there was a sliver of cognition that remembered the garden. The memory was faint but insistent: the shining gazebo, the liquid-gold pond, the unconditional love. She attempted to speak, to tell the doctors and nurses about her experience, but only disjointed words emerged.

In the following hours and days, Amber's condition remained grave. Doctors marveled at her partial awakenings, but they also recognized the enormity of her stroke. She required extensive monitoring, therapy, and medication to keep seizures at bay. She drifted in and out of consciousness, sometimes feeling as if she were hovering between two worlds. When she finally stabilized enough for physical therapy, she grappled with every challenge imaginable: learning to move her right arm and leg again, practicing how to swallow without choking, and struggling to form sentences. Each victory, no matter how small, was overshadowed by the sense of how far she still had to go.

Her emotional and spiritual recovery proved equally tumultuous. Initially, Amber felt as though she was a burden to her family. She had spent her adult life caring for others, but now she needed help walking from one end of the room to the other or even feeding herself. The stress took its toll, exacerbated by anti-seizure medications that muddled her thoughts. Outbursts of frustration turned to tears. She sometimes questioned the veracity of her NDE, wondering if it was just a vivid hallucination brought on by trauma. Why, she asked herself, would she be sent back to a body so broken?

But her family rallied around her. Her husband, recalling the vow he'd made when he stood beside her in the helicopter, remained her unwavering support, sleeping in a hospital chair night after night. The children visited daily, offering embraces and laughter that momentarily soothed her worry. The foster kids, too, stepped up—cooking meals, tidying the house, and sharing encouraging stories about the difference Amber's presence had made in their lives. Slowly, day by day, the love that anchored her to life began to reaffirm her decision.

After weeks in medical facilities, Amber was cleared to go home, though she faced months—if not years—of challenging rehabilitation. Therapists visited daily, guiding her through exercises to strengthen her limbs and coax her speech back into fluid expression. She spent hours relearning tasks as basic as combing her hair or typing a text message. Meanwhile, her psychic gifts intensified. She found she could sense others' physical and emotional states more keenly than ever before, as though the stroke had peeled back another layer of spiritual awareness.

At first, the sheer volume of energy and emotion around her was overwhelming. Entering a grocery store or riding in a crowded car triggered bouts of anxiety as she felt every flicker of stress from the people around her. However, with practice, counseling, and support from fellow intuitives, Amber learned techniques for grounding and shielding. She rediscovered her center, weaving her newfound clarity into her professional offerings as a medium, psychic, and healer.

Gradually, the predictions her guides shared in the garden became manifest in her day-to-day life. While the first six months post-stroke were indeed painful—marked by tears, self-doubt, and seemingly endless therapy—she began to see how her journey was helping those around her. Clients who heard her story found hope in knowing that miracles do happen, that even catastrophic strokes can yield spiritual awakenings. People who had doubted life after death took comfort in hearing Amber's testimony of her heavenly garden, its undeniable love. They recognized that for all her astonishing gifts, Amber was, at her core, a human being who had suffered and chosen to fight her way back.

As for her family, the shared ordeal drew them closer. Gone were the everyday squabbles about whose turn it was to set the table; in their place arose deeper bonds of mutual care. Her children saw in their mother a model of resilience and grace, and they became kinder not only to her but to one another. Even the extended foster family came together in the wake of Amber's stroke, forging a sense of community that transcended conventional definitions.

Amber looked back on her stroke not as a curse, but as a pivotal chapter in her soul's evolution. She eventually referred to it as a gift, albeit one wrapped in pain and trials. It had crystallized her life's purpose: to be a conduit of healing, love, and spiritual insight for others. It pushed her to reexamine the meaning of life and the preciousness of every moment. Far from dismissing her near-death experience, she now embraced it as the guiding star that illuminated her path.

When people asked if she would change anything, Amber often smiled gently. "I wouldn't trade what happened," she would say. "It brought me back to the essence of who I am and why I'm here." In simpler words, the stroke—and her fleeting glimpse of that celestial garden—rekindled her commitment to serving as a bridge between worlds: the physical realm where human connections matter so dearly, and the spiritual realm where love is eternal and infinite.

In time, her story spread beyond friends and family. Fellow stroke survivors found motivation in her remarkable recovery; struggling parents saw in her the proof that resilience can blossom in even the most trying circumstances. Aspiring mediums reached out, hoping to learn from someone who had navigated that luminous garden and returned with a profound message of hope.

And Amber, for her part, continued to use her gifts—sight, intuition, empathy, healing—to help those who sought guidance or needed solace. She noticed how the lines between her professional calling as a social worker and her spiritual calling as a medium blurred in the best possible way. Clients left her sessions not just with solutions to tangible problems, but also with a sense of the grander tapestry of existence, assured that each life is stitched into an intricate design far surpassing human understanding.

No one could look at Amber's life and call it ordinary. She juggled the usual tasks of motherhood—grocery shopping, helping with homework, folding laundry—while in the same breath offering messages to grieving families from their departed loved ones, or quieting the anxiety of a frightened cat. Always, she recalled how easily she could have stayed in that divine garden, letting earthly struggles fall away. Yet the pull of love for her family had been stronger, and she had chosen to return.

In that choice, she had embraced both her hardships and her purpose. And every time she remembered the garden's shimmering light, its flowers pulsing with life, and the kind smiles of Gail and Jessica, Amber felt waves of gratitude for the second chance she'd been granted. She had walked to the brink of death, seen the vastness of eternity, and stepped back with a promise she intended to keep: to share her truth, to uplift others, and to affirm that, no matter how dark the night, love always stands waiting, radiant and unwavering, just beyond the veil.

———

TWO
BILL DOLAN

TV PRODUCER DIES AND ENCOUNTERS
GOD AND ETERNITY; WHAT HE WAS
TOLD WILL SHOCK YOU

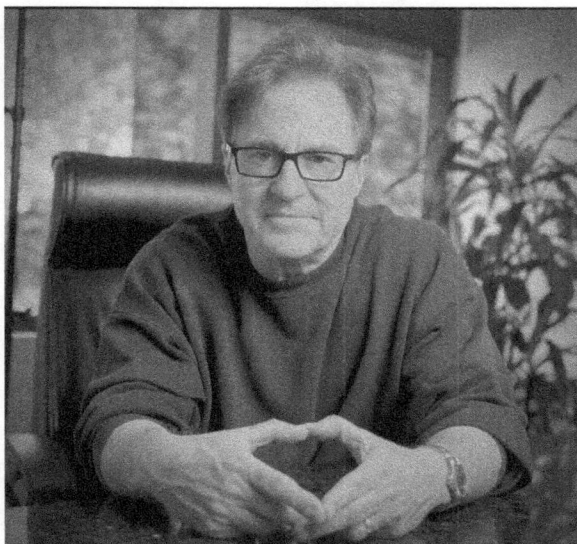

Bill Dolan, a TV director whose life was forever changed
when his heart stopped mid-flight to Nashville. Bill was
traveling to secure a lucrative deal for a new documentary
project when the unimaginable happened. The profound

encounter with the divine that followed transformed his life in ways he never expected. What he learned on the other side will leave you speechless. Stay tuned to hear Bill's extraordinary journey from death back to life and the powerful message he brought with him.

———

January 28, 1999, would remain etched in Bill Dolan's memory as a day that utterly transformed him—a day he discovered that all of life could pivot in the span of a few heartbeats. Back then, Bill was a man riding high on professional success, balancing his career as a television director and producer at a prominent network with the family life he'd once dreamed of. He was known for his genial demeanor, quick wit, and an uncanny ability to find a story in even the most ordinary situations. But behind that confident exterior lay the struggle and self-doubt of a man who feared he was losing the most precious parts of his world.

Bill had been a storyteller for as long as anyone could remember. As a boy, he would gather his siblings in the living room of his parents' home, weaving tales inspired by the novels he devoured or the films that sparked his imagination. His father's bookshelf overflowed with history, biography, and the occasional thriller. Bill pored over all of it, enthralled by the heroes, villains, and moral quandaries he discovered. When other children were outside climbing trees, Bill often preferred to be inside, devising elaborate dramas with action figures or spinning ghost stories for neighborhood friends. The worlds he created felt more vivid to him than everyday life. He saw narratives everywhere—a cloud formation, a piece of old furniture, even an abandoned baseball glove could spark a grand adventure in his mind.

As he grew older, Bill's creative spark found focus in television production. In college, he majored in communications and visual media, determined to bring his visions to life on a larger stage. His professors noted his extraordinary drive; he wasn't merely fulfilling assignments—he was pushing boundaries, experimenting with techniques, and staying up late to perfect transitions or sound mixes. This dedication earned him early internships, then minor roles at a local station, and finally an opportunity to direct segments for a national network.

Professionally, Bill's rise came with exhilarating speed. By his late twenties, he found himself in the midst of high-pressure live broadcasts, coordinating camera angles and cutting in real time, while millions watched from their living rooms. He thrived on this adrenaline, felt entirely alive in those moments when every shot mattered. Through determination and talent, he rose through the ranks and became a sought-after director for large-scale TV productions.

Despite his career accomplishments, Bill Dolan's personal life carried a quieter tension—one largely hidden from his colleagues. He had married his high school sweetheart, Margaret, a patient, compassionate woman who had stood by his side since they were teenagers. Together, they had built a family, welcoming four children into their hectic world. Margaret was the anchor of the household: she cooked meals, kept track of school schedules, and offered unwavering emotional support. Whenever Bill's work required him to be away—often far too long—she absorbed the additional load with stoic grace.

Deep down, Bill was haunted by guilt. Each time he returned home late from the studio, he'd find Margaret tidying up the remnants of dinner or tucking the children into bed. Sometimes she would put on a brave face, asking how his day went, but Bill sensed the weariness behind her smile. She never complained outright; her silence was more potent than any words of reproach could be. He told himself he was doing it all for them—to provide a stable life, to give his kids the opportunities he'd never had. Still, as nights of missed bedtimes, weekends away, and incessant phone calls stacked up, Bill felt as though he was losing something precious. Precious moments slipped away—first words, first steps, triumphant soccer wins, and heartfelt late-night conversations—all missed in the relentless pursuit of professional success.

It was after the birth of his youngest child that Bill first felt the stirrings of a deeper discontent. Holding his newborn daughter in his arms, he was overwhelmed by a sense of awe and love so fierce that tears rolled down his cheeks. Her tiny hands, her soft breath, the warmth of her body— these were irreplaceable treasures. He looked at Margaret, whose gaze reflected both joy and quiet fatigue, and realized he had to make a change. He vowed to find a better balance, to be the husband and father his family deserved.

In an unexpected twist of fate, a friend from the motion picture industry approached him to collaborate on a documentary. This project held tremendous appeal for Bill: it wasn't bound by the rigid, frenetic timeline of live television, and it could allow him to invest himself in a slower, more meaningful creative process. He met a like-minded collaborator in a gospel singer and music producer named Timothy Granger. The two men bonded quickly, drawn together by their shared passion for storytelling and the conviction that media could be a force for good in the world. Though Bill still had plenty of professional commitments, he found genuine excitement in this new venture— and the possibility of being home more often.

By January 1999, Bill and Timothy's documentary was in full swing, demanding but fulfilling work. It centered on the depths of human experience, exploring themes of love, sacrifice, and faith in ways that resonated profoundly with Bill's own longing to reconnect with life's most important values. In the midst of all this, Timothy managed to secure a meeting with a distributor in Nashville who seemed poised to help them take their documentary nationwide. The trip felt momentous to Bill, like an answer to his silent prayers for a more balanced, purposeful path.

On the morning of January 28th, Bill boarded a flight to Nashville with Timothy by his side. The mood was buoyant. They chatted about their pitch, rehearsed their talking points, and envisioned the possibilities for what they could achieve. Bill felt certain this meeting could launch him onto a new trajectory—one where he could unite his storytelling flair with his yearning to stay closer to his family.

Roughly twenty minutes into the flight, Bill noticed a tingling sensation in his fingers. He flexed them, thinking he might be cold or anxious, but the tingling spread up his arms and into his chest. It felt as though a band tightened around his ribcage, restricting his breathing. A sudden wave of dread rolled over him. He glanced at Timothy and murmured, "I don't feel right."

Those four words would be the last he spoke before his eyes rolled back and his body went limp. His heart stopped, and Bill Dolan, the director known for orchestrating productions before millions of viewers, now teetered on the edge of life and death, slumped in an airplane seat tens of thousands of feet in the air.

At first, Timothy thought Bill was joking, perhaps feigning a faint in a moment of casual banter. But it took only seconds for him to realize something was terribly wrong. Panicked, he shouted for help. The flight attendants rushed down the aisle, bringing an AED (automated external defibrillator) and oxygen, while Timothy, who had no formal CPR training, instinctively began pressing on Bill's chest. Around them, passengers looked on in shock—some praying, others frozen in fear.

Time slowed. Timothy remembered feeling each second stretch out like an eternity as he prayed for a miracle. He pleaded for Bill's life, tears stinging his eyes. The flight attendants worked urgently to stabilize the situation, coordinating with the pilots to arrange an emergency landing. For precious minutes, Bill's heart did not beat on its own.

Then, suddenly, Bill's chest heaved. A faint gasp of air escaped his lips, and his eyelids flickered. Chaos gave way to trembling relief. Timothy shouted, half-laughing, half-crying, as Bill weakly regained consciousness. The plane hastily diverted, landing at the nearest airport. Paramedics rushed aboard, transferring Bill to a waiting ambulance and speeding him to the nearest hospital. There, doctors uncovered the cause of his cardiac arrest—a rare neurological condition called neurocardiogenic syncope. In Bill's case, it was malignant: his brain sporadically sent signals that stopped his heart. Without medical intervention, another such episode could be fatal.

As doctors implanted a pacemaker to regulate Bill's heartbeat, he drifted in and out of awareness. Though sedation and confusion clouded his recollections, he clung to fragments of an experience that words struggled to convey. He remembered no sense of fear, no swirling darkness. Instead, he recalled stepping into a realm of boundless love and light. In that place, every fiber of his being felt embraced—seen entirely, accepted without conditions. For a man who had grown up feeling God was distant or judgmental, this divine intimacy shattered every preconceived notion. It was as if pure love permeated every cell of his existence.

When Bill's heart stabilized and he regained full consciousness, his first thought wasn't about the meeting in Nashville or even his own brush with death. Instead, he was consumed by the memory of the love he'd felt on the other side. Through tear-filled eyes, he tried to explain it to Timothy and the doctors. He stumbled for words, comparing it to stepping into eternity, a feeling of indescribable warmth and light coursing through him. As news of his survival reached Margaret and the children, Bill's hospital room became a hub of tearful reunions and hushed gratitude.

Over the days that followed, his physical strength returned, but the Bill Dolan who left the hospital was not the same man who had boarded that plane. His life was no longer just about career milestones or professional acclaim. He realized that every breath was precious—that time with loved ones was both fleeting and infinitely important. He yearned to hold his children close, to tell them stories at bedtime, to be there for small, seemingly insignificant moments that truly made up the tapestry of life.

The sense of urgency Bill had once reserved for elaborate TV broadcasts now shifted to creating deeper relationships. He listened more attentively, laughed more freely, and savored an unspoken closeness with his wife that only came from surviving a crisis and finding renewed perspective. Rather than diving right back into an unforgiving work schedule, he allowed himself the space to recover spiritually as much as physically.

Before long, Bill found that sharing his story was part of his healing. At first, he spoke quietly to close friends and mentors—a pastor at church, a couple of longtime colleagues who visited him during recovery. They reacted with awe and curiosity, asking him to describe the love he'd felt. Each time he tried, he was reminded of how inadequate language could be for expressing something transcendent. Yet he persevered, believing that even incomplete words of testimony might offer hope to someone grappling with despair or fear.

In time, Bill began receiving invitations to speak at local community groups, colleges, and small conferences. People wanted to hear about the day his heart stopped on an airplane and about how he had returned with a different view of life's priorities. He recounted how, during those moments of death, all material concerns and petty ambitions melted away, leaving only love—love of God, love of family, love of creation. One day, as he addressed an audience of fellow media professionals, he noticed tears shining in their eyes. It dawned on him that every person, no matter how successful or worldly they seemed, harbored some longing for that kind of acceptance and grace.

Margaret watched her husband's transformation with quiet wonder. She saw him turn down projects that would have kept him away from home for weeks. She noticed how he made eye contact with each of their children, asking about their days, their dreams, and how they felt about life. He no longer wanted to be the father who hovered on the periphery of their lives; he wanted to step into it fully, cherishing every grin, every scraped knee, every bedtime story.

Professionally, Bill didn't abandon his passion for story-telling. But his motivations shifted radically. He still directed and produced, but now his choices centered on projects that aligned with the truths he had discovered. He poured himself into the documentary he'd begun with Timothy, weaving in deeper themes of faith, purpose, and compassion. It became not just a film but a testament to the power of human resilience—something far beyond a mere paycheck or an industry accolade.

Whenever Bill thought back to that airplane cabin, he remembered how quickly life could change, how unexpectedly one could be forced to confront mortality. On the day his heart stopped, an entire flight of strangers had become witnesses to his brush with death. Some had prayed, others had wept, and Timothy had physically fought to keep him alive. The memory humbled Bill, reminding him of the interconnectedness of human beings. It reinforced the notion that love—whether it arises in an emergency or in everyday moments—can bridge divides and save lives in more ways than one.

Though his miraculous survival story spread among colleagues and within his community, Bill kept a humble stance. He often said, "I'm no hero; I just got a second chance." He considered his newfound lease on life a gift from a gracious Creator who had touched him with a love so vast it defied earthly comprehension. He discovered that faith, at its core, was less about religious dogma and more about a personal relationship with the source of that boundless love.

For Bill Dolan, the events of January 28, 1999, marked the stark dividing line between his old life and his new life. Before that day, he had chased success, trying to create a name for himself in the frenetic world of broadcasting.

After that day, he became a man committed to living authentically, savoring the smallest joys, and sharing his testament of grace and second chances.

Looking back years later, Bill would sometimes reflect on the chain of events that led him to his seat on that plane. He recognized how near he had come to never seeing Margaret's smile again, never hearing his children's laughter echo down the hall. Yet he emerged from that near-fatal moment with not just a pacemaker, but a recalibrated heart in a spiritual sense. To him, it was both a rebirth and a vow: to devote his talents, his energy, and his love to what truly mattered.

His story became a powerful reminder that every heartbeat can be a threshold to revelation. In one instant, Bill died— and in that brief, infinite moment, he was flooded with a love that would guide the rest of his days. He carried it back into the world, determined to live a life defined not by deadlines and accolades, but by compassion, humility, and a devotion to his family. For all who encountered him —friends, colleagues, strangers—Bill stood as proof that life's greatest miracles often happen in the blink of an eye, but their reverberations can inspire others for years to come.

———

THREE
DAVID DITCHFIELD
HE DIED IN A TRAIN ACCIDENT AND MET HIS GUARDIAN ANGEL; WHAT HE WAS TOLD WILL SHOCK YOU

David Ditchfield faced a life-altering accident that led him to an otherworldly realm. After being trapped by a train, David was pulled under its wheels and experienced a miraculous near-death experience. In this divine realm, he encountered healing lights and guardian angels, inspiring him to create profound art and music that gained widespread recognition.

———

On a cold, gray afternoon in February of 2006, David Ditchfield made his way through the bustling Cambridge train station, his breath escaping in small puffs that swirled in the icy air. The ancient cobblestones outside were slick with winter dampness; inside, the station was alive with voices, footsteps, and the echo of train announcements. David was in no particular rush that day—he was there for one simple reason: to see his close friend Anna off on her trip. Neither of them had the faintest idea that this routine goodbye would transform David's life forever.

At first glance, there was little about David that seemed out of the ordinary. He wore a thick, worn-in sheepskin coat that fought off the February chill. He was tall and had an earnest way about him, though those who looked closely might have detected a subtle heaviness in his eyes. In the months leading up to that day, he had been struggling with a sense of restlessness. There had been financial problems, creative blocks, and the lingering feeling that life wasn't quite lining up the way he'd once imagined. Anna's friendship was a ray of light in an otherwise stressful time and seeing her off was as much about a moment of companionship as it was about courtesy.

Their conversation was casual as they ambled onto the platform. Anna teased David about the perpetually chilly weather in Cambridge, and he joked that he should be living somewhere closer to the equator. Their laughter blended into the familiar background noise: train doors slamming, briefcases clicking, the shuffle of people going to and from the city. When Anna's train arrived, it hissed to a stop, its doors whooshing open in a chorus of mechanical beeps. Passengers poured out, merging with the crowd on the platform, some greeting loved ones, others rushing on their way.

A few minutes remained before departure, so David and Anna chatted at the doorway of the train. Their breath mingled in the cold air, and the station's fluorescent lights gave everything a faint, buzzing glow. Anna was excited for her trip—she was going to see family in London—and David felt a genuine warmth in wishing her well. He gave her a hug, patting her on the shoulder, and promised to catch up soon. She stepped inside, found a seat, and turned to wave at him one last time.

Then came the moment that would change everything.

The automated buzzers sounded, indicating the doors were about to close. David reflexively stepped back from the train, intending to give the doors clearance. But in that instant, the thick hem of his sheepskin coat became wedged between the closing doors. He felt a sudden, immobilizing tug that jolted him out of the ordinary. Panic flared like a spark in his chest. He yanked at the coat, but the train's mechanism had already locked onto it. He pulled again—harder this time. Nothing budged.

Inside the train, Anna realized with horror that David was caught. She pressed her palms against the glass door, her eyes wide, and shouted for someone to help. She tried to yank the emergency lever near the door, but the train was already gearing up to move, and no guard appeared to halt its motion. David's heart slammed against his ribs as he looked up and saw the train wheels beginning to turn. A metallic groan rose from the rails, and he knew with icy clarity: If this train leaves the station, I won't survive.

David yelled for help, hoping someone on the platform would jump into action. A few people noticed—some even ran toward him—but in a chaotic instant, the train jerked forward, picking up speed much faster than David expected. The powerful momentum yanked him along, causing him to lose his balance. He skidded sideways across the platform, boots scraping the concrete. He could hear Anna's muffled screams from inside the train, but they were drowned by the rush of wind and the thunderous roar of the engine.

His coat's robust fabric had become his worst enemy, refusing to tear, refusing to let go. As the train moved beyond the platform's edge, David's foot slipped into the narrow gap between train and platform. His balance vanished, and he found himself dragged into that perilous space. He would later describe it as being "swallowed by a metal monster," a moment of raw terror in which every second felt impossibly stretched. A cacophony of grinding rails, clanging metal, and his own racing thoughts consumed him.

The train continued to accelerate, pulling him along the side. It seemed unstoppable—an iron beast on a fixed path, oblivious to the human being trapped against its flank. David felt his body smash into the hard edge of the platform and then tumble free onto the tracks. Adrenaline, pure and scorching, flooded his system. One fleeting thought cut through the chaos: Fight to live.

Somewhere in that desperate struggle, either the coat finally tore, or the door clamp gave way—he never knew which. Suddenly, he was released, tossed like a rag doll onto the gravel between the rails. The train thundered on overhead, so close that its metal undercarriage rumbled just inches above him. David pressed his face to the ground, gravel digging into his cheek, as the final train cars roared past. He could barely register the pain at first—his senses were overloaded by the enormous violence of the event.

At last, the train disappeared into the distance, leaving a vacuum of silence on the platform. Bystanders stared in stunned disbelief. Then, like a bursting dam, everything happened at once: shouts, frantic phone calls to emergency services, people rushing to help. David lay immobile, gasping, trying to make sense of the fact that he was still conscious, still alive. His left arm was mangled, blood pooling beneath him. His legs felt like lead, and every breath came with sharp, stabbing pain. Yet, a small, persistent part of him was shocked to find himself breathing at all.

Help arrived with startling speed. Paramedics ran onto the tracks with a stretcher, carefully lifting David's battered body. The sharp edges of the gravel seemed to tear at every nerve, and he winced as they maneuvered him. He caught glimpses of alarmed faces, hushed voices barking commands, bright orange uniforms. In that blur of motion and pain, David felt his mind begin to slip into a haze. The paramedics hoisted him into an ambulance, and he listened distantly to someone explaining that they had to rush him to a specialized trauma center if he stood any chance of keeping his arm—or even surviving.

He began to fade in and out on the ride to the hospital, the sirens wailing in his ears. Time seemed fluid, melting into pockets of confusion. At one point, he heard a voice telling him they still had a 25-minute drive. At another, a doctor inside the ambulance asked him to stay awake, to keep talking. David's answers were slurred, but the fear in his chest grew with each bump and turn of the vehicle. He kept thinking of Anna's face behind the train window, her eyes filled with terror.

When they finally arrived at the hospital, the medical team swarmed him like a pit crew at a race. Cool fluorescent lights glared overhead as he was wheeled at breakneck speed down a long corridor, doors swinging open and snapping closed behind them. David could hear urgent conversations about blood loss, surgery, and the necessity of removing his coat and clothes to see the full extent of his injuries. The smell of antiseptic stung his nostrils. A surgeon's face appeared above him, urgently inquiring if David had family to call.

A moment later, Anna appeared, pale and trembling, tears streaming down her cheeks. She whispered shakily, "They said on the station speakers that someone had died. I thought it had to be you." Her fear-laced eyes met his as the medical staff prepped him for emergency surgery. David tried to respond, but his throat felt constricted. He managed only a faint nod, his head swimming with shock.

And then, as the intensity peaked—monitors beeping, voices colliding—David felt an incredible sense of calm wash over him. The edges of his vision blurred, and he sensed himself drifting away, as if gently slipping out of his body. Before he fully registered what was happening, the hospital room dissolved, replaced by a vast, dark void. However, this darkness was not cold or empty; it was profoundly peaceful.

He felt weightless, free from the gravity of his broken body. No more cold, no more pain. He found himself strangely content, even curious, as he gazed into the velvety blackness. Slowly, points of light began to materialize in the distance, shimmering in an array of hues— amber, green, yellow, red. They pulsed like living stars, radiating warmth and something akin to love. The lights drifted around him, drawing closer in a mesmerizing dance.

In the soft glow, David discovered he was lying on a massive granite rock. A supple, blue satin sheet covered his body. Astonishingly, he felt no injuries. His limbs were intact, his pain vanished, replaced by a humming sense of wholeness. He looked up to see geometric grids of white light forming overhead, their perfect symmetry descending toward him like a grid over a map. With every inch they moved closer, he felt a profound healing energy. It was as if gentle hands were massaging his spirit, dissolving old wounds—physical, emotional, and spiritual.

Then, he sensed a presence at his feet. Turning, David saw a being made entirely of light, neither male nor female, standing there with an indescribable warmth emanating from it. He felt instantly safe. Two more beings appeared, one on each side, each sending what felt like loving pulses toward him, causing every cell in his body to vibrate with an overwhelming sense of love. In that moment, David understood these beings to be guardians or guides, ancient souls aligned with his own journey.

Rather than the frantic thoughts he'd had in the hospital, he now felt an indescribable serenity. A life review flashed behind his eyes—memories of childhood struggles, lost opportunities, the quiet heartbreaks he rarely spoke about. Yet, there was no judgment here. He sensed only compassion, a gentle nudging that suggested he was loved in spite of every shortfall. Then, a series of scenes unfolded— people he cared about, unresolved hurts, moments he wished he could redo. The love he felt made him realize that these regrets were invitations to grow, not burdens to condemn himself for.

Next, he was shown a waterfall—though it wasn't water cascading, but an infinite stream of stars. Trillions of points of light shimmering in a cosmic curtain, as if the universe itself was pouring out its brilliance. The sense of unity he felt at this vision was almost too large for words. He belonged to it, and it belonged to him. The boundaries between "self" and "all" blurred, expanding into a single harmonious flow.

Finally, a great tunnel of incandescent light appeared, rimmed with flickers of flame that might have been symbolic or literal—he couldn't quite tell. The energy pouring from it carried an impossibly powerful love, so intense that David found himself laughing out of sheer joy and relief. He recognized this glowing expanse as the source of all creation, something he might have called "God," yet it was unlike any deity he had learned about. It was pure, radiant love, formless yet encompassing everything.

David yearned to merge with that love, to fully enter it and never return. But just as he moved closer, a firm yet gentle voice spoke: "This is not your time. You have to go back." He felt himself resisting, clinging to the freedom he'd discovered, but the message repeated, compassionate yet unyielding: "Not yet. You must return to complete your purpose."

In an instant, the celestial realm vanished. He snapped back into the harsh fluorescent glare of the hospital. Alarms beeped, doctors murmured instructions, and he felt excruciating pain flood his senses. The transition was so sudden it took his breath away. His battered body screamed with agony, yet beneath the physical suffering, he sensed a lingering calm—the echo of that boundless love he had just experienced.

Over the next several hours, David underwent a marathon surgery—eight and a half hours in total. He drifted in and out of consciousness, each time remembering fragments of that other world. When he finally stabilized, the doctors told him how close he had come to losing his life. They were amazed he had survived, much less retained function in his limbs.

As days turned into weeks, David's body slowly mended, but his mind and spirit were propelled into a new chapter of existence. He found himself replaying the images of the lights, the granite rock, the star-waterfall, the indescribable love. Despite having no prior artistic training, he felt a magnetic urge to paint what he had seen. He acquired large canvases and let the colors flow from his brush. To his astonishment, the images that emerged felt guided by an unseen hand. The shapes, the hues—they brought the other realm back to life in vivid detail.

He also discovered an unexplainable drive to compose music. He had never considered himself a musician, yet melodies formed in his mind as if dictated by those same light-beings he'd encountered. Eventually, he completed a piece he called The Divine Light, and, through a series of remarkable coincidences, it was performed by an orchestra. The audience, many of whom knew little of David's story, were moved to tears by the composition's depth and beauty.

Year by year, David's life expanded in directions he never thought possible. He sought out spiritual communities and circles, including a local spiritualist church, to better understand his experience. He learned that many others had undergone near-death experiences (NDEs) and that his was far from unique—yet uniquely his own. He began speaking about his ordeal in podcasts and interviews, eventually writing his memoir, Shine On, despite grappling with dyslexia. With a friend's help, he shaped his memories into a written testament of survival and awakening. The book was released just before the pandemic, and it quickly found a global readership, resonating with those seeking solace, courage, or simply the hope of a second chance.

Today, David often reflects on the hardest lesson from his NDE: returning to the physical world when every fiber of his being wanted to stay in the light. Yet, it's a lesson that has guided his daily life ever since. He strives to live more fully in the present, cherishing the small details of human existence—warm sunbeams, laughter shared with friends, the textures of paint beneath his fingers, the wondrous fact of breath entering and leaving his body each moment.

His arm still bears scars from that fateful day in February 2006, and at times he has flashbacks of the train station's chaos. But in those scars and memories, he sees echoes of transformation rather than trauma. Through painting, composing music, and sharing his story, he channels what he experienced in that realm of light. He reminds others that even in the darkest hours—whether trapped in a personal crisis or literally dragged by a speeding train—there is still the possibility of unimaginable love and a profound sense of purpose waiting on the other side.

David Ditchfield's life is thus a tapestry woven from tragedy and transcendence. What began as a routine day ended in blood and heartbreak, yet it also led him to witness a boundless universe of love and healing. His art, his music, and his memoir serve as living proof that the human spirit can be shattered and rebuilt, forever changed by the grace glimpsed in a single, extraordinary moment. And for those who listen to his story or view his creations, there is a reminder that life's greatest challenges can become portals to a deeper reality—one in which compassion, creativity, and connection are the pillars that hold us upright, no matter how hard the winds may blow.

———

FOUR
DEBBIE ALI
KIDNAPPED AND TORTURED FOR 14 DAYS; SHE DIED AND MET GOD.

Debbie Ali, a published author and trauma counselor, recounts her extraordinary journey of survival and spiritual awakening. On her 31st birthday, Debbie experienced a harrowing home invasion on the small island of

Trinidad, leading to her abduction and captivity for two weeks. Throughout this ordeal, Debbie endured unimaginable horrors, including physical assaults and near-death experiences. Her story takes a remarkable turn as she describes an out-of-body experience where she encounters a divine presence and receives a profound message of hope and resilience. This powerful narrative explores Debbie's transformation from victim to survivor, her encounters with the divine, and her ongoing mission to help others who have experienced trauma. Her story is a testament to the strength of the human spirit and the enduring power of faith.

———

Debbie Ali never thought of herself as someone who would come close to death in such a horrific way. She grew up in a devout Christian household on the small Caribbean island of Trinidad, developing a passion for words early on. Writing short stories and devouring books became her way of making sense of the world. In time, her empathetic nature led her to counsel others, especially women dealing with trauma. She became a published author, ghostwriter, and eventually a counselor to those suffering from PTSD.

She married and had two children, an eight-year-old and a six-year-old, who brought her immeasurable joy. On December 5, 2006—her 31st birthday—she expected a peaceful day. Her children, along with her husband, left home, hinting at plans to surprise her later. In the meantime, Debbie occupied herself by tidying the house, indulging her love for the Christmas season. She opened the garage door for a brief ten minutes at most, feeling relatively safe with neighbors and road workers around. Yet unease stirred when she realized they had left. She moved to close the garage door.

In an instant, her world turned upside down. Two masked men, one wielding a machete and the other a gun, stormed in, overpowering her. A cold fear seized her heart as the muzzle pressed to her temple. They dragged her away from her home, forcibly pushing her into a waiting vehicle. Hours later, the police and an anti-kidnapping squad discovered that Debbie had been abducted, but for reasons unclear, her captors kept her for two weeks—much longer than the typical "snatch and ransom" pattern on the island.

During those two weeks, her husband negotiated for her release, though it remained a mystery why the ordeal was so prolonged. Debbie's captors inflicted unimaginable brutality: they starved her, beat her, and even set a pit bull on her. The pit bull attack left her scarred physically, but the relentless trauma pushed her body and mind to the brink. Chained to a bedpost, her wrists handcuffed and her feet tied with rough straps, she was permitted only two short, humiliating showers. She fought to keep her eyes open during the worst beatings, terrified that giving in to the mounting shocks and blackouts might mean her end. Each morning she clung to faith, reciting prayers and recalling comforting passages from the Bible.

By the eleventh or twelfth day, her body was nearing total collapse. Her mind, however, began using mental coping techniques to survive. She focused on her children, envisioning them safe at home. Still, the unrelenting pain and uncertainty left her convinced she could not endure much longer. One morning, feeling exceptionally weak, she sensed her guard had stepped away. An overwhelming heaviness weighed on her, and she teetered on the edge of consciousness. The pain finally melted into numbness, and she felt herself exiting her body.

In a surreal shift, Debbie realized she was floating above her battered form. She saw the dark, grimy room as though with new eyes, noting details she hadn't been able to perceive while blindfolded. She recognized she was dead, but the fact carried no fear. Instead, she felt profound compassion for her own injured body and recollected every piece of her identity—her name, her children, her life. Down below, the woman she once was lay limp, scars testifying to two weeks of vicious abuse.

In that suspended state, a brilliant white light approached, so intense yet not blinding. It flooded her with a warmth that dispelled all lingering pain or fear. Emerging from the light was Jesus, unmistakable in identity, though not conforming to any single depiction she'd seen in art or church. She dropped to her knees at his feet, noticing they were bare like hers, glowing with a luminous energy at the toes. She felt more complete than she ever had in life, an overwhelming relief and gratitude surging through her.

Jesus lifted her gently, allowing her to rest against him. She felt like a child in his arms, every ounce of tension and sorrow draining away. Moments later, she realized they stood on a boundless beach. The world around them pulsed with colors indescribable in Earthly terms. There was no sun, yet everything radiated an intrinsic glow. She sensed God's presence permeating all things: the sand, the water, the air itself. Peace beyond comprehension enveloped her.

They began to walk along the shore, communicating telepathically. Jesus emanated endless compassion, letting her know her earthly pain was understood. Then they reached an even brighter white light—the presence of God. The voice of God, sweet and resonant, filled Debbie with awe. Jesus asked if she truly wanted to return to the living, and she cited her children as her reason. He replied that they would be looked after, but her insistence remained strong: she yearned to be there for them, to guide them.

To her surprise, Jesus showed her a vision of a book titled "Bare Feet." She grasped that she was to write it and share God's message: "I see all, I hear all, I know all that happens in the darkness and the light." Jesus blessed her in that moment, healing her battered spirit and endowing her with renewed strength. As they walked back along the shoreline, she saw everything—fish, waves, even the very air—still itself in reverence to his presence.

When it came time to leave, two archangels, Michael and Gabriel, appeared at her sides to guide her journey back. A group of saints, including Abraham, Moses, Jacob, Mother

Mary, and Elisha, prayed fervently for her. Mother Mary's gaze carried an assurance that every mother's prayer finds its way to God. Debbie curled into a fetal position on the sand, and in an eye-blink, she was back in her kidnapped body, the full agony of her injuries rushing back to her senses. The clarity from the heavenly realm, however, lingered in her consciousness, fueling her resolve.

Shortly thereafter, her captors chose to accept only part of the ransom and free her. One of them, who had caused her terrible harm, had softened after hearing her words of faith and forgiveness. He felt conflicted, urging her to escape; but she, recalling divine instructions, worried for his safety if she fled without caution. Ultimately, they decided to drop her from a moving vehicle to finalize her release. Dazed but functional enough, she managed to call her husband, who traced the call. That night he found her, weeping with relief, in an emotional reunion reminiscent of biblical deliverance from bondage.

The aftermath was far from simple. The kidnapping left deep psychological scars. Debbie struggled with PTSD, facing depression and flashbacks. Her body carried wounds that would take much time to heal. Despite the recurring nightmares, a radiant memory of Jesus and that beach in Heaven served as her anchor. She began telling her story almost immediately—though fragile, she felt compelled to testify about the love and comfort she experienced, convinced it might offer hope to others.

In the years that followed, Debbie gravitated toward helping other women cope with the ripple effects of violent trauma. She leveraged her personal insight: the mental resilience strategies she used in captivity, the unconditional forgiveness she granted her captors, and the knowledge that a higher love awaits beyond mortal tribulation. Late at night, she often found herself answering calls from strangers—women in crisis who needed a steady voice telling them that rescue was possible, that God and angels might be nearer than they imagine.

She never forgot the divine instruction to write a book— "Bare Feet"—to share God's message. While grappling with daily stresses, she pursued writing projects, ghostwriting for clients, working on screenplays, and incorporating her own experiences into pages meant to uplift others. Through every setback, she clung to the promise that she had something important to accomplish.

Her faith, once a simple daily devotion, evolved into a deeper spirituality that encompassed angels, saints, and the abiding presence of Jesus. She spoke candidly about how Earthly ambitions and material concerns fade in the face of raw survival and the afterlife's reality. During her captivity, no possession could have saved her, but love, faith, and a determination to see her children again carried her through. In that ultimate crisis, it was God's unwavering gaze and Jesus's supportive arms that reminded her human life, for all its pains, is sacred, infused with meaning beyond our immediate comprehension.

Publicly, Debbie reiterated the message: "Money can come and go. Your homes and status can vanish overnight. But the love you nurture, the kindness you practice—these linger, continuing beyond death's threshold." Now in her daily pursuits—be it counseling a battered mother or writing a new book chapter—she aims to radiate the compassion she felt in that beachside moment in Heaven. Where once she might have faltered under the weight of bitterness, she now stands resolute, a living testament to survival and the boundless possibility of renewal.

Though echoes of fear still visit her in nightmares, Debbie believes that God will never forsake her—and indeed, never forsakes anyone. She has endured extreme brutality, but in that bleakness, she found the brightest light. By sharing her experiences, she hopes others will discover paths to resilience, forgiveness, and a steadfast knowledge that, beyond the darkest corners, a radiant love awaits those who choose to trust it.

is Debbie Ali. I am a published author, ghostwriter, and screenplay writer. I've also done extensive counseling, especially with women who have suffered trauma and PTSD. This career path was influenced by the story I'm about to share, my near-death experience, which occurred on my 31st birthday, December 5, 2006.

On that day, I was home alone on a small island called Trinidad in the Caribbean. My two young children, aged eight and six, had gone out with their father to plan a surprise for my birthday. I stayed home, indulging in my love for Christmas by doing some cleaning. I had left my garage door open for no more than five or ten minutes while I worked. Although I felt relatively safe with neighbors and road workers around, I decided to go back inside when I noticed them leaving.

Within seconds of turning my back to close the garage door, two men invaded my home. They were masked, one holding a machete and the other a gun. They quickly overpowered me, and I felt an immediate cold fear as a gun was pointed at my head. They abducted me from my home and held me captive for two weeks, which completely baffled the police and the anti-kidnapping squad because hostages are usually held for no more than a week without a ransom being paid.

During those two weeks, while my husband was negotiating for my release, I endured unspeakable brutality. I was beaten, starved, and even mauled by a pit bull. I went into shock several times, felt the onset of it, and struggled to stay alive. I was handcuffed to a bedpost and my feet were tied with straps. In those dark days, I saw no light and was allowed only two showers.

Growing up as a devout Christian, I never gave up hope. Around the eleventh or twelfth day of my captivity, I used mental techniques to cope with the stress and trauma, techniques I now teach other women. Despite these efforts, my body was weakening. One morning, when my guard left, I felt an overwhelming sense that I wouldn't make it. As I drifted into what felt like a deep sleep, the pain began to fade, and I felt myself separating from my body.

Suddenly, I was above my body, still aware of who I was and my memories of my family. I looked down at myself and saw the room where I was held, despite being blindfolded for two weeks. I even drew the room later in hopes it would help the police. Realizing I was dead was not intimidating or scary, it was a mere statement of fact.

As I hovered over my body, an incredible white light approached me. I looked directly into it without any discomfort. The light brought an overwhelming sense of peace and bliss. Jesus stepped out of the light, and I immediately recognized him. I felt so humbled that I dropped to his feet, which were bare like mine, since I had been abducted without shoes. The light emanated from his toes, and I felt complete just being at his feet.

Jesus lifted me up, holding me like a newborn baby, and told me it was okay to rest. I snuggled into his arms and felt an unparalleled sense of comfort. When I woke up, still in his arms, I found myself on the beaches of Heaven. The colors were beyond anything on Earth, and the peace was indescribable. Everything around me was vibrant, and there were no shadows. The light surrounded every object, and Jesus explained that there was no need for a sky because God encompassed all things.

We communicated telepathically as we walked along the beach. Jesus eventually led me to an even more brilliant white light, out of which came God's voice. God's voice was the sweetest sound I had ever heard. Jesus asked why I wanted to go back, and I said it was for my children. He assured me they would be taken care of better than I ever could. He then showed me a vision of a book titled "Bare Feet," which I was to write to deliver his message to the world: "I see all, I hear all, I know all that happens in the darkness and the light."

Jesus blessed me, healing all my injuries, and filled me with strength. As we walked back, the water and fish stood still in his presence. When it was time to return, Archangel Michael and Archangel Gabriel were placed by my sides to protect and guide me. Saints, including Abraham, Moses, Jacob, Mother Mary, and Elisha, were also there, praying for me. Mother Mary smiled at me, conveying that God always answers a mother's prayers.

I curled up in a fetal position on the sand and, in what felt like the blink of an eye, I was back in my body. The pain returned, but I knew I would be okay. My captors accepted a fraction of the ransom money and released me. The kidnapper who had brutalized me became my protector after I taught him about Jesus. He begged for my forgiveness, which I granted. He even tried to help me escape, but I chose to stay to save his life, as God had instructed.

Upon my release, I was thrown from a moving vehicle, but managed to call my husband, who traced the call and rescued me. The reunion with my family was deeply emotional. I immediately began speaking publicly about my experience, driven by the purpose Jesus had given me.

Life has been difficult since then, dealing with PTSD and depression. However, the memory of Jesus holding me and the promise of heaven keeps me going. I've counseled many women, often late at night, to help them through their own traumas. My near-death experience taught me that life is precious and how we treat people is even more so. Money is less important than the love and kindness we show to others.

———

FIVE
DEBRA MARTIN
SHE DIED IN A CAR ACCIDENT AND WAS SHOWN THE TRUTH ABOUT GOD AND MIRACLES

Debra Martin, a certified research medium, shares her extraordinary journey from childhood encounters with spirits to multiple near-death experiences that ultimately led her to become a healer. After a car accident on the night of Princess Diana's death, she received a premonition that saved her life and experienced a divine intervention. Another NDE saw her communicating with a divine being who guided her through a transformative spiritual journey. Battling a mysterious illness and later cancer, Deborah witnessed miraculous healings facilitated by spiritual surgeons. These profound experiences solidified her faith and purpose, empowering her to heal others worldwide with her unique gift, blending divine guidance and love.

———

Debra Martin's life began in an unassuming neighborhood, where the days were sunny and carefree—yet the nights were anything but ordinary. From the time she could form her first memories, she experienced vivid and startling visions that set her apart from other children. At the tender age of four, when most kids dreaded shadows or the boogeyman under the bed, Debra encountered far more concrete fears. Each night, long after her parents had tucked her in, she would find herself lying rigid beneath the covers, staring into the dark. Except she wasn't truly alone. Strange figures—spirits—moved about her room with an uncanny clarity. They appeared as distinct forms, not fuzzy apparitions that vanished when she blinked. She could see the contours of their faces, sense their presence, even feel the slight shifts in the air.

To a young child raised in a practical household, the encounters were terrifying. There were no bedtime stories about angels or guides, no older family member gently explaining that these visitors were guardians or lost souls. Instead, her parents—especially her mother—assumed these ghostly sightings were born of nightmares or imagination. Night after night, Debra would gather her courage and call for help. "Mommy, can I come downstairs?" she would plead. But the grown-ups had long days behind them, and more often than not, she'd receive a calm dismissal: "It's just your imagination. Go back to sleep."

For Debra, hearing that her reality was nothing but fantasy felt deeply isolating. She would clench her eyes shut, listen to the hollow silence of the house, and try to will away the shapes gliding through her room. It was a lonely struggle —one in which she received no comfort or validation. Eventually, it became too overwhelming. One night, mustering all her childish courage, she whispered a command to the spirits: "Go away. I don't want to see you anymore."

The next morning, she awoke to a strange quiet. The shadows hadn't reappeared. The sense of watchful presence was gone. Amazingly, her blunt request had driven them off.

Little did she know, she hadn't destroyed her gift; she had merely pressed pause. Debra grew up with no further supernatural disruptions. She busied herself with school, friendships, and the ordinary concerns of childhood. Summers passed in a flurry of family vacations, bike rides, and late-night giggles with friends. Winters brought snowy afternoons and the coziness of holiday gatherings. Nothing about her outward life suggested that she had once interacted with a realm beyond what most people perceive.

As Debra entered adolescence, then adulthood, she married, had children, and settled into routines of carpools, grocery lists, and the trials and triumphs of raising a family. To any neighbor peering over the fence, she was just another devoted wife and mother. Beneath the surface, however, the universe was stirring, inching her toward moments that would test her faith, her resilience, and ultimately reveal the dormant abilities she had once suppressed.

Her first near-death experience (NDE) arrived in 1997, during a time fraught with global grief. Princess Diana had just died, and the world seemed to hold its collective breath in mourning. Debra, out with friends, felt a somber aura overlay their usual laughter. The conversation repeatedly touched on the princess's tragic accident. By the evening's close, Debra found herself wrestling with unease when a friend offered her a ride home in a sporty, low-slung car. Something inside her—an intuition or an inner voice—whispered that she should stay behind or find a different ride. But she brushed it off, telling herself she was just being emotional due to the sad headlines.

They headed onto the freeway, the hum of the engine blending with the subdued chatter in the car. Suddenly, a jolt of certainty surged through her: they would crash. The feeling was absolute, as if someone had flipped on a switch in her mind. Her heart hammered, and she opened her mouth to speak, to warn her friends—but she never got the chance. Within seconds, the car lost control. Tires screeched in protest, and the vehicle spun like a top on asphalt before slamming into a guardrail. Metal shrieked as it crumpled, and Debra felt the impact reverberate through her body. Doors bent inward, trapping them inside.

Panic set in, everyone calling out, adrenaline spiking. Then, in the midst of the chaos, a man appeared. Neither Debra nor her friends saw him approach, but there he was —calm, collected, and inexplicably powerful. He seized the bent metal of a door and, with what seemed like super-human strength, pulled it open. His presence exuded a strange serenity that steadied Debra's breathing. One by one, he guided each passenger out of the wreck. When it was Debra's turn, his hand on hers felt warm and reassur-ing. As soon as the paramedics arrived, she turned to thank him—and realized he was gone. No one recalled seeing him walk away, and he didn't linger to provide a name. The rescue workers had no explanation. Debra, shaken and thankful to be alive, mulled over the notion that this stranger might have been an angel in disguise.

In the months that followed, Debra gradually left the memory of that night behind. Life is relentless in its forward march, and responsibilities at home overshad-owed introspective musings. Yet the experience planted a tiny seed: a thought that divine intervention was real, that there was more to existence than what met the eye.

The second NDE struck during a seemingly routine day. Debra was out running errands, an unremarkable chore that ended abruptly in a terrifying collision. She was in her car at an intersection, turning left, when another driver barreled forward, suffering a diabetic seizure that rendered him oblivious to traffic signals. He slammed into Debra's car with monstrous force, twisting metal like tinfoil. The wreck was catastrophic, and by all logic, fatal.

But Debra didn't experience the collision in a straightforward way. One moment she felt the impact, the next she was floating above her shattered vehicle. Below her lay crushed steel, shattered glass, and the limp body she realized was hers. Oddly, she felt no fear or pain—only an encompassing clarity. A figure of pure, radiant light stood behind her, emanating warmth that bathed Debra in calm. She sensed the figure's question echo in her mind: *"Are you ready to leave?"* Images of her children flashed like a rapid slideshow, each face dear and irreplaceable. She responded without words, but with unshakable resolve: *"No."*

In a blink, she was back in her body, lungs burning as she inhaled, aware of paramedics and onlookers screaming about how miraculous her survival was. The medics called it "divine luck" or a "miracle," though no one could quite articulate how she had escaped with her life. Recovering physically from this accident was a challenge—bruises, internal pain, doctor visits—but Debra soon realized that an even deeper spiritual shift was underway. She had glimpsed a realm beyond the physical and returned to tell the tale.

Years rolled on, peppered with the highs and lows of family life. Debra didn't anticipate that her hardest battle was yet to come. Inexplicable bouts of pain began invading her daily routine. At first, they were intermittent—nags of discomfort that she tried to dismiss. But they grew relentless, morphing into a chronic torment that flared without warning. It seemed no part of her body was spared. Doctors scratched their heads, prescribing pain medication or ordering tests that revealed nothing conclusive. Desperate for an explanation, Debra traveled to the esteemed Mayo Clinic, where the best specialists examined her. Time and again, their findings were inconclusive. The relentless agony persisted.

Emotionally spent, she faced despair. Unable to sleep, too exhausted to find joy in simple tasks, Debra prayed for an end to it all. If relief meant death, so be it, she told the universe. One night, the pivotal moment arrived. Lying in bed, she sank into a state that felt both dreamlike and hyper-real. She opened her eyes to an astonishing sight: a room teeming with translucent, glowing figures—what she later called "spiritual surgeons." Unlike her childhood experiences, these beings appeared purposeful, methodical. She felt their cool, precise touch as they performed what seemed like a supernatural operation on her abdomen. The pain was excruciating, as if knives were cutting through flesh, and it was too much to bear. In response, her consciousness lifted away from the agony, floating above her body as these surgeons continued their intricate work.

In the next heartbeat, she was transported to a realm of unearthly light. It wasn't a typical near-death tunnel or a lonely expanse; it felt warm, nurturing—like being wrapped in a cosmic embrace. Then came an even brighter entity—one she instantly recognized as God, though she couldn't explain how. He held her broken earthly body, placing it gently on a luminous beam beside a strange glass-like coffin. Leading her into a grand dome structure, He showed her a contract, lines of text and symbols glowing with significance beyond words. It detailed her life purpose and revealed that she'd already overstayed her initial allotment of time on Earth.

Softly, God offered her a choice. She could finalize her departure or reaffirm a mission she had yet to complete—a mission that would require returning to her ailing body but with renewed purpose and healing. The enormity of this decision weighed on Debra. Trembling, she chose life. She felt her spirit "sign" the contract without pen or paper, an act sealed by her deepest will.

No sooner had she made her choice than she was plunged back into her physical form. The sensation was akin to being inflated from within, like a balloon quickly filling with air. She jerked awake, heart pounding, pain still present but somehow different—as though the grip of her illness had loosened. Over the following months, her health improved at a pace that defied reason. Blood tests confounded doctors, who maintained there was nothing to diagnose, even as they witnessed her miraculous turn-around. In silent prayer, Debra asked God why nothing showed up in the tests. His reply echoed in her mind: *"Because if there had been a diagnosis, you would have owned it."*

Emboldened by this transformation, Debra realized that her spiritual senses—dormant since childhood—were reawakening. Once more, she began to see beyond the physical, sensing spirits and energies. This time, she embraced her abilities rather than sending them away. She trained herself to channel divine healing, engaging in prayerful meditations and guided visualizations that seemed to tap into a universal source of love and life force.

Word spread in her circles that Debra Martin had a "gift." Over time, people with various ailments—physical, emotional, spiritual—sought her help. She began practicing "distant healing," a method where she focused her healing energy on someone miles or even continents away. Astonishing recoveries followed. One of the most notable stories featured a close friend battling tongue cancer. Debra dedicated sessions to pray and visualize the friend's throat bathed in white-gold healing light. Doctors soon found that the tumor had diminished remarkably, leaving them baffled and labeling the improvement "unexplained."

Encouraged by these results, Debra pursued formal recognition of her mediumistic and healing abilities. She became a certified research medium at the Windbridge Institute, a pioneering organization that scientifically studies mediums and afterlife communication. This role allowed her to provide comfort to families longing to connect with deceased loved ones. When she relayed intimate details from the beyond, details she couldn't possibly have guessed, hearts broke open to new possibilities: that consciousness persists beyond death, that love truly transcends the grave.

Yet, life had another test to administer. During a routine moment of self-awareness—an intuitive check she felt prompted to perform—Debra discovered signs of anal cancer. The blow rattled her. After all she had been through, after her miraculous healings, how could she face another battle against a life-threatening illness? She recognized, however, that her prior experiences had been preparing her for exactly this test. Leaning on medical intervention alongside prayer and unwavering faith, Debra underwent chemotherapy and radiation. Every day, she practiced gratitude, meditated on restoration, and leaned into a deep trust that the divine was with her. She emerged from the ordeal not unscathed but strengthened—her conviction unbreakable.

Today, Debra's life is a rich tapestry, woven from encounters with the unimaginable—moments of deep despair that sparked transformative spiritual insight. She sees her life as a testament to how adversity can spark deeper understanding, how the fragility of our bodies can highlight the endurance of our souls. More than once, she's teetered on the edge of life and death and returned with stories of angelic intervention, near-death revelations, and metamorphic healing.

A central pillar of her teaching is the boundless potential of hope. She reminds people that, no matter how dark the situation appears, we possess an innate power to connect with the divine—whether one calls that God, Source, or

Higher Consciousness—and that through this connection, miracles unfold. Her own saga underscores the principle that faith, combined with determined action, can alter trajectories once believed set in stone.

Debra also emphasizes love—the most universal language —as the key to unlocking this healing potential. In her healing sessions, whether she's physically laying hands on a person or praying at a distance, love acts as the conduit, bridging the gap between the human and the divine. She offers the assurance that even in the face of medical diagnoses, unrelenting pain, or devastating accidents, there is a wellspring of grace available if one remains open and trusting.

In the end, Debra Martin's story is not only about surviving catastrophes; it's about embracing the extraordinary truths that lie hidden in plain sight. It's about shedding the veneer of fear to reclaim the gifts we once shunned, whether they be psychic abilities or simple faith. It's about forging a partnership with the divine that can animate our days with purpose, healing, and unshakeable hope. Her journey reminds us that life is far more expansive than the confines of our five senses—that, indeed, each of us has the power to defy darkness, transcend our scars, and heal in ways we never deemed possible.

———

SIX
JANICE CALLAHAN
WOMAN DIES FROM OD; MEETS GOD AND IS TOLD THE PURPOSE OF LIFE AND OUR SOULS

Janice's near-death experience began with a drug overdose that caused her body to shut down and her spirit to hover, terrified, between life and death. In that critical state, she sensed herself separating from her physical form, fully aware of each organ failing. Suddenly, she found herself in a place bathed in a shimmering, opalescent color, where tall, translucent beings stood to her left, and an immense, loving presence—whom she recognized as the Father—permeated her entire being. Although she felt fully seen and known, there was no condemnation, only sorrow for time wasted. She was then transported to a second scene in bright daylight, where countless people stood shoulder to shoulder, and she received a clear command from the divine presence: *"Love them."* Accepting this mission and understanding she must tell the truth of her ordeal without changing herself, she was briefly merged into the Father's love in an indescribably unifying way before snapping back into her body. Gasping for air, she felt overwhelming warmth coursing through her and found herself speaking a foreign language, fully convinced that the power she had encountered was real—and that love was the ultimate answer.

———

Janice Callahan often looked back on the year 2018 as a turning point that completely reshaped her life. For years she had wrestled with bouts of depression, periods of hopelessness, and occasional substance misuse. Still, she had never truly imagined that a single night could bring her face-to-face with death in a way so profound it would challenge all her assumptions about life, love, and the nature of reality.

That fateful evening began like many others—unremark-able at first. Janice found herself with a companion whose presence she had been seeking for distraction and escape. She had used drugs before, sometimes to manage pain, sometimes to dampen emotional turmoil, sometimes simply out of habit. This evening, however, something different happened. The usual haze that dulled her senses was replaced by an acute, terrifying awareness that she had gone too far.

Her body felt wrong. She couldn't breathe properly, as if invisible hands gripped her throat. She coughed and gasped, desperate to pull air into her lungs, but each breath became more labored. Her heart hammered in her chest with explosive force—until it suddenly seemed to slow, leaving her mind spinning with a single realization: I'm dying.

Amid the suffocating panic, Janice also felt an odd hyper-clarity. Chemicals surged through her system in a chaotic storm; it seemed like her own cells were at war. She knew she was edging into the danger zone—past the point where her body could rebound on its own. In the blur of adrenaline, she remembered the man beside her helping her onto a couch, elevating her feet as though that might somehow stave off the crisis.

Time began to distort. Seconds felt like minutes, minutes like hours, and yet the entire ordeal later proved to have lasted only a short while. Janice pleaded silently, Please don't let me die... please let me live... She had struggled with depression before—countless days in which she saw no meaning in her own existence—but faced with this very real threat of death, something inside her cried out for a chance to keep going.

She felt her spirit detach, as though part of her hovered near the ceiling of the living room. Through a panic-stricken haze, she squeezed the man's hand as if it were an anchor to this reality. She couldn't hear him speak, couldn't tell if he was aware of her condition, only that 911 was never called. The hush in the room clashed with the storm inside her body. She realized that she was on the cusp of leaving life behind if something didn't change immediately.

Then, in a flash that she would never forget, her awareness snapped off and on again—only to find herself in a place utterly unlike the living room she had just been in. The transformation was startling, like stepping through a hidden door. She opened her eyes to a realm tinted in a soft, shifting color between gray and lavender, an opalescent shimmer that moved like ripples on water. The very air seemed alive, electric with a gentle glow.

To her left stood three beings. Their outlines were human-like—tall, upright—but they were translucent, as if carved from the purest light. Janice instantly recognized them as angels, though they spoke no words. Their presence carried a warm gravity. One angel reached out a hand toward her, and in that moment, she knew with crystalline certainty that taking it would seal her fate in that realm. It would mean accepting death.

Every fiber of her being resisted that choice. She wanted to go back, to remain a mother to her children, to right her mistakes. Her heart ached with regret over wasted years, foolish risks, and the possibility that her youngest child might grow up without memories of her. She felt wholly known and entirely loved by these angels, yet she couldn't bear the thought of leaving her children behind.

A presence even more immense than the angels then filled her awareness. Towering, powerful, and drenched in love, it radiated a compassion so vast it made her feel both small and absolutely cherished at the same time. Though it was invisible as a form, she sensed it was masculine—like a father. A force field of love pulsed from him, coursing through her in waves. She thought of divinity—of God, of Jesus—and felt gratitude well up in her for the sacrifice she believed allowed her to be in the presence of such grace.

She began to plead. Images of her children flooded her mind, particularly her youngest daughter, who was too small to carry any lasting memories of her mother. In breathless urgency, she begged, Please let me return. I can't die now. Not like this. No voice answered her in words, yet the divine presence enveloped her with understanding—unconditional acceptance, no judgment, no condemnation.

At that moment, everything shifted again. She found herself under a brilliant sun, outside, standing on a raised platform next to that same immense, loving presence. Before her stretched a countless number of people, packed shoulder to shoulder, all gazing up at her. Their expressions were neutral, almost blank, as though waiting for a cue. She felt an unspoken understanding that she was supposed to do something for them, or with them, but she had no idea what.

She asked in her mind, What do I do? and leaned on the presence for support. The response came in a gentle wave, as if communicated directly to her heart: Love them. Such a simple directive, yet so profound. With an inward rush of relief, she realized it was something she could do—indeed, something she desperately wanted to do. If there was any chance at all she could go back to the living world, she would dedicate herself to love.

But her next question was more complicated: What do I say? On a deeper level, she wondered if she would have to admit the full truth of how her life had spun out of control, or how she had come to be in this situation. The response was immediate: Tell the truth. She cringed at the thought, embarrassed by how her decisions might appear to others, but she also felt a powerful sense of relief at the instruction.

Then she asked, What do I need to change? The presence replied, Nothing. In that one word, Janice sensed multiple meanings. It was not telling her to remain stagnant but assuring her that transformation would come through honesty and love, not through her own forced attempts at perfection. The presence indicated that it would guide her, that she need only speak openly and let the natural process of growth unfold.

She thought about the crowd, noticing no single person stood outside or away from the mass—every individual was equally included. She grasped that this presence offered love to all in equal measure, that no one was favored or excluded. Everyone was waiting for hope, for love, for whatever message she had to share.

Finally, she wondered how she would learn what she needed to fulfill this commission. The response resonated through her spirit like a bell: It's already inside of you. Whether the presence meant wisdom, compassion, or divine insight, she understood it to mean that the seeds of understanding were already planted deep within her soul.

In a heartbeat, she found herself back in that first, shimmering realm—the lavender-gray environment with the three angels. But now she felt light, relieved, certain she was about to return to her life. She floated in a sense of euphoria. Then, as though someone had opened a channel between her heart and the vast expanse of unconditional love, she felt herself melt into the divine presence. It was like being absorbed into pure love on a cellular level.

She caught a glimpse of her hand—transparent and light—but with an unshakable sense of reality. She realized that humans were threefold beings, composed of body, soul, and spirit, and it struck her how perfectly they interwove. As this revelation stirred her thoughts, scenes from her past, especially moments of trauma and sorrow, surfaced. Yet here, in this space, the sting of those memories vanished. She understood the events, the people involved, and her own reactions with a clarity that erased shame and pain.

Curiously, she perceived other souls as well, going about their own lives. They did not see her or even realize they were enveloped in this immense field of divine love. The sense of unity with all living beings deepened her awe: We're all held here, she thought. We just don't know it.

Then, with sudden force, she was pulled back into her body. She inhaled so sharply it felt like her lungs might burst. She found herself once again on the couch, staring into a familiar living room—only now everything was colored by wonder. She gasped and began to speak, trying to exclaim, The answer is love! Jesus is real! Everything is true!

Her companion stared at her with wide-eyed shock, as though he had witnessed a ghostly resurrection. Janice noticed she was sweating, her body seized by a potent heat that rose from her core like a surge of fire. Yet it did not harm her. Instead, it felt purifying, as if every cell in her body was igniting with new life.

When she tried to speak again, the words tumbled out in a language she did not recognize. Her mind was forming English sentences, but her mouth produced unfamiliar sounds. The man next to her appeared both frightened and perplexed, confirming that she was indeed speaking in something other than English—some unknown language that poured out in a flood.

Over the weeks and months that followed, Janice's life transformed. Gone were the daily battles with hopeless-ness, replaced by an unwavering conviction that she was loved, guided, and profoundly connected to others. She felt compelled to share her story, no matter how vulnerable it made her. *"Tell the truth,"* the presence said, and Janice would do just that, taking it as her sacred mission in life.

Whenever she spoke of her near-death experience, her words overflowed with the memory of that overpowering love. She shared how she had seen angels, how she had felt a fatherly presence that offered only compassion, how she had touched a realm where no pain existed. She insisted that the environment itself had been made of love, a living substance that permeated everything.

Janice also recounted how, in that space, there was no condemnation—only a gentle sadness for wasted time, for letting herself become ensnared in harmful habits. She believed wholeheartedly that the presence wanted her to return, to tell others that life was more precious than they might ever realize. It was time, she felt, to stop running from the truth and to start embracing the love that held them all.

Those who listened to her story often sensed the change in her, noticing an openness and tenderness that hadn't been there before. She no longer hid her struggles with addiction or her lapses into depression. Instead, she spoke openly about them, confident that honesty was part of her calling. "I was instructed to love," she would say. "And the only way I can show that love is through truth—about who I am, what I've done, and how I came to see what really matters."

Her reunion with her children became a profound moment of healing. Each time she tucked her youngest daughter into bed, she would remember that moment of terror in the overdose—fearing she'd never see her child again—and renewed her gratitude. She now approached motherhood with reverence, determined to pour out the love she had experienced into every interaction, every hug, every bedtime story.

As the months rolled on, Janice sought out ways to help others who were trapped in their own cycles of drug abuse or despair. She volunteered at a local shelter, eventually speaking publicly about her near-death experience. Some people responded with skepticism or dismissal, but many more found hope in her words. Several reached out to confide that they, too, had felt the whisper of something greater, the sense that love was the ultimate foundation of life—even if they had never seen it so clearly.

Janice believed that no one was beyond redemption and that everyone, no matter how isolated or broken, was embraced by the same divine presence that had welcomed her. She also believed that the directive to "tell the truth" meant not only being transparent about her past but also reminding others that they were inherently worthy of love —even if they couldn't see it in themselves.

To those closest to her, Janice often described the intangible aspects of her experience: the shimmering lavender-gray light, the angels' gentle invitation, and the colossal presence that made her feel both tiny and infinitely valued. "It's not something I can prove," she would say, "but it's something I can't deny." She maintained that within that loving presence, there existed a profound equality—no one person was more cherished than another.

In quieter moments, she reflected on the transformations in her own body and mind—how the mysterious fire that coursed through her seemed to wash away layers of self-destructiveness. She had emerged with a clear awareness of the threefold nature of human existence—body, soul, and spirit—and how deeply connected all people were to one another within that boundless field of divine love.

Even years later, small details from that night continued to resonate. She remembered the couch, the faint smell of the room, the man's stunned face, and her own frantic last pleas for life. But more than anything else, she remembered the presence's calm voice: *Love them. Tell the truth. You don't have to make any changes by yourself—I'll guide you through it.*

She often ended her recollections the same way: by affirming that every day was now a gift. "If I can return from the brink of death, carried by divine love, then there's hope for all of us," she would say. "No matter how dark things seem, no matter how lost you feel, love is real. It's what we're made of, what we live in, and what unites us all."

And for Janice, this had become the truest thing she had ever known.

———

SEVEN
JEFFREY OLSEN

MAN DIES IN CRASH; DISCOVERS TRUTH ABOUT GUILT AND FORGIVENESS IN EMOTIONAL NDE

Jeffrey Olsen was an ordinary man whose life changed irrevocably when a tragic car accident claimed his wife, Tamara, and their youngest son, Griffin. Although he survived, badly injured and consumed by guilt, he experienced vivid near-death encounters that showed him the power of unconditional love and a profound oneness with all people. Guided by Tamara's radiant presence, he felt compelled to return for his surviving son, Spencer, and later underwent a harrowing recovery that tested his physical and emotional limits. Through a sequence of spiritual insights—encounters with divine light and a deep sense of acceptance—Jeffrey discovered that even in great loss, there is a greater capacity for growth, gratitude, and compassion. He carries this lesson with him, living with intention and reminding others that, ultimately, love is all that truly matters.

———

Jeffrey Olsen grew up in the rolling foothills of northern Utah, where the mountains cast long shadows across the farmland each evening. His parents owned a modest family farm, a place of early mornings and chores that demanded discipline, patience, and a practical mind. Even as a child, he preferred feeding chickens or tending fields over seeking the limelight. Although his parents divorced when he was young, the lessons of perseverance and self-sufficiency left an imprint on his heart, shaping a perspective that would serve him both practically and spiritually in years to come.

As he entered adulthood, he traded the rigors of daily farm life for more creative work in marketing and advertising. Colleagues admired his calm, dependable manner, while clients trusted that if Jeffrey made a promise, he would keep it. Over time, he met Tamara, a high school teacher with a nurturing spirit. She had grown up in southern Utah—land of striking red rock canyons and imposing arches—and carried a warmth that drew people in. Their marriage blended two grounded individuals who found joy in building a supportive, loving home.

Ten years later, they were raising two boys: Spencer, seven, and Griffin, just 14 months old. Spencer brimmed with imagination, forever staging elaborate action-figure scenarios. Griffin, still toddling, had wide, curious eyes and a sweet disposition. The couple counted their blessings: they had once been told a second child might be impossible, yet here Griffin was, a tiny miracle. Life felt bright, rooted in simple routines—Jeffrey's agency work, Tamara's teaching job, and their children's daily adventures.

One spring, Easter approached with a chill in the air, and Tamara suggested a long weekend in southern Utah to visit her parents and grandparents. The family packed their SUV with snacks, sweaters, and Spencer's fleet of action figures. As they drove south, the landscape transitioned from pine-lined mountains to desert plains and finally to the crimson canyons that Tamara knew so well. They spent the weekend attending big family breakfasts, wandering around local rock formations, and watching Spencer delight in a backyard Easter egg hunt. Griffin toddled about under watchful eyes, enthralled by the new sights.

On Monday, despite reluctance, they needed to return to their routines in northern Utah. The family lined up on the front porch to wave goodbye. Jeffrey strapped Griffin into his car seat, and Spencer clambered in beside him. Tamara settled into the passenger seat, and Jeffrey turned the key. Just as he began to pull away from the curb, Tamara suddenly said, "Wait! Stop!"

He braked, assuming she had left something behind. Instead, she hopped out and ran to her parents, hugging them both and planting a tender kiss on each cheek. She did the same with her grandparents. Although Jeffrey felt they were already running late, he watched with a mixture of mild impatience and deep fondness as Tamara, beaming, returned to the car. She took his hand, and they waved one last time at the smiling family on the porch.

They set off on a drive of four to five hours. Jeffrey nudged the cruise control up to 75 miles per hour, determined to reclaim at least part of his workday. Tamara reclined her seat and drifted to sleep, still loosely holding Jeffrey's hand. Spencer entertained himself in the backseat, creating epic battles with his toys, while Griffin dozed off in his car seat. At one point, Jeffrey glanced in the rearview mirror and lingered on the sight of Griffin's tiny form, noticing for the thousandth time how long his eyelashes were. He listened to Spencer's excited chatter, felt Tamara's hand in his, and thought, "How did I get this lucky?" That moment felt timeless, overflowing with gratitude.

An hour later, everything changed in the blink of an eye. The SUV veered to the right. Whether Jeffrey dozed or reacted to something on the road, he could never be certain. In a reflex, he swerved too hard to the left, losing control. The vehicle began to roll along the highway with sickening force, flipping end over end. Witnesses would later say it rolled six or eight times. During most of this, Jeffrey blacked out. When the SUV finally stopped, the smell of gasoline and twisted metal overwhelmed him. He was pinned, unable to move.

Through the roaring in his ears, he heard Spencer screaming. The boy was alive but hysterical. Jeffrey tried to reach him, only to discover he could not move at all; he was trapped in the mangled wreckage. Then the horrid realization fell over him: he heard no other cries. Neither Tamara nor Griffin made a sound. In that desperate moment, he sensed they were gone. Overwhelming grief seized him, alongside excruciating physical pain. His legs were shattered—one so badly it would later require amputation above the knee—his back broken, his right arm almost torn off, and his internal organs severely damaged. Gasping for air, he slipped in and out of consciousness, tormented by guilt that he had been the one behind the wheel.

Just when it seemed nothing could pierce his despair, Jeffrey felt a sudden presence of radiant light. It washed over him like a gentle tide, softening the agony and making breathing easier. It was as though he were leaving his body; he felt himself rise, gaining a new perspective from above the crumpled SUV. Looking down, he recognized his own broken form pinned in the driver's seat. Then Tamara appeared by his side in that same glowing space, radiant and unhurt. She communicated, without words, that Spencer still needed him. "You can't stay here," she insisted. "You must go back." Jeffrey understood in an instant that he had a choice—but there was no real question. If he stayed, Spencer would be alone. He said goodbye to Tamara in a rush of heartbreak and love before feeling himself pulled away from that peaceful realm.

He next found himself drifting through the halls of a busy hospital. Doctors in white coats and nurses in scrubs dashed around. Anxious families waited in corridors. Strangely, no one noticed him, but he noticed them in profound detail. Whenever he passed a person, he instantly knew them—sensed their fears, their joys, the very fabric of who they were. This oneness was so all-encompassing that it defied his previous understanding of human connection. Every being seemed woven together by threads of unconditional love.

Then he saw a body on a gurney, surrounded by the urgent efforts of medical staff. It appeared lifeless, injured beyond belief. Drawing closer, he realized with shock that it was his own body. At the mere thought—"I need to go back into that body"—he felt a sudden, overwhelming pull. In a flash, he was awake in his physical form, slammed by the overwhelming pain, sorrow, and haunting knowledge that Tamara and Griffin were gone.

Later, he would learn that some hospital staff had mystical experiences of their own. A doctor and a nurse described seeing a beautiful female presence above Jeffrey's bed, radiating gratitude, as though she were silently thanking them for saving her husband. Jeffrey had, of course, been somewhere else in those moments, but the reports matched his own sense of Tamara's involvement in his survival.

The next few months proved grueling. Jeffrey underwent multiple surgeries to remove his shattered left leg, reattach parts of his right arm, stabilize his broken spine, and repair internal injuries. In moments of unbearable pain, he felt his spirit lift from his body, as if granting him respite from the relentless torment. Grief also descended in waves; in quiet nights between nurse check-ins, the loss of Tamara and Griffin seemed too much to bear.

Amid those trials, Jeffrey experienced another profound near-death-like event. One night, he finally fell into a deep, peaceful slumber. He became aware of the same comforting light and suddenly found himself in what he could only describe as "home." It was a realm of indescribable beauty, alive with color and warmth. Here he had two strong legs and felt boundless energy. He ran and laughed, filled with a sense of joyful freedom.

Intuitively sensing he was not there to stay, he followed a corridor that appeared before him. At the end of that passage stood a crib—the one Griffin had slept in as a toddler. Rushing forward, he peered in and saw Griffin lying there, just as peaceful and radiant as ever. With tears in his eyes, Jeffrey picked up his son, holding him close, feeling the warmth of his small body.

A divine presence enveloped them from behind, a cosmic love that transcended all human understanding. Fearing judgment, Jeffrey braced himself, painfully aware that he had been driving the car. But this presence communicated only unconditional love. He heard, without hearing words, that there was nothing to forgive, that all was in divine order, and that life was about learning from each experience. Scenes from his past swept by—childhood struggles, mistakes in adulthood—yet each was met with a loving invitation: "What did you learn? Who have you become because of it?"

Then came a pivotal moment. The presence let him exercise free will regarding Griffin. Jeffrey could keep clinging to his son, or he could surrender him to God, trusting in the greater plan. Sobbing, he pressed his lips to Griffin's brow and released him, giving his child over to divine care. Instantly, he found himself back in his hospital bed, awakened once more to the practical realities of braces, amputations, and medical tubes. Yet he felt changed— somewhere inside, a fragment of peace had taken root.

When he was finally discharged, his brothers helped him into a wheelchair and drove him to the home where Spencer had been staying. Jeffrey worried endlessly about how his son would react to seeing him so incapacitated— missing a leg, covered in scars, and dependent on others. As they pulled into the driveway, Spencer flew out of the house, sprinted across the yard, and ran right past Jeffrey's wheelchair. For a disheartening moment, Jeffrey believed the boy couldn't handle it.

But then Spencer's shouts rang out: "Come out, come out! My dad has made it home! Come see my dad!" He was knocking on neighbors' doors, proudly announcing his father's return. Before Jeffrey could even process it,

Spencer dashed back and flung himself onto his father's lap, hugging him fiercely. Despite the jolt of pain, Jeffrey felt tears rush to his eyes. He tried to explain that he might never be the same, but Spencer looked at him with absolute devotion and said, "Dad, if you were nothing but a puddle of blood, I would still love you."

That moment captured the very heart of the lessons Jeffrey took from his near-death experiences. Over the years, he has come to believe that life is a gift, not a test. He has seen that humanity is connected in ways deeper than most ever perceive, and that at the root of everything lies unconditional love. Even grief, he says, is evidence of love for someone cherished so deeply.

Though his physical body carries scars, prosthetics, and the lingering aches of trauma, his spirit feels taller and clearer. He seeks to show kindness to strangers, to value every fleeting second with those he cares about, and to honor Tamara and Griffin by living wholeheartedly. He and Spencer, now grown, share a bond forged by shared loss and strengthened by unwavering love. They keep the memories of Tamara and Griffin alive through stories, laughter, and annual tributes on special days.

Wherever Jeffrey goes, he encourages people not to wait until some terrible wake-up call to appreciate the preciousness of life. He suggests they reach out to others, speak words of love more often, and remember that the simplest moments—watching a sunset, enjoying a hot cup of coffee, or feeling a friend's warm embrace—are nothing short of miraculous. He hopes everyone can recognize that beyond the boundaries of this world lies a love that embraces all souls, a bond that remains unbroken even by death.

To this day, Jeffrey maintains that if his experiences have taught him anything, it is that all there is, in the end, is love. It extends beyond injuries, beyond grief, beyond the physical separation of life and death. It ties every person together in the deepest oneness imaginable, and it can heal wounds that once seemed insurmountable. He lives each day with gratitude, holding tight to the truth that even in sorrow and loss, love endures—and so does hope.

———

THE OTHER SIDE NDE
YOUTUBE CHANNEL

Ebook readers, click on image above to view channel trailer.

The Other Side NDE, explores and shares the fascinating stories of near death experiences (NDEs) from people all over the world. Our mission is to provide a platform for individuals to share their experiences and insights, and to raise awareness about the transformative power of NDEs.

We believe near-death experiences hold the power to profoundly transform lives and broaden perspectives. Our carefully curated collection of videos features firsthand accounts from individuals across diverse backgrounds and life paths. Each story is distinct, offering a powerful glimpse into the mysterious and often transformative nature of NDEs.

We understand that the topic of NDEs can be sensitive and personal, and we respect the privacy of our contributors. Our videos are carefully edited to ensure that our contributors feel comfortable sharing their experiences with the world.

If you have experienced an NDE, we would love to hear from you. Please get in touch with us through our Submit Your Story page to share your story and join our community of individuals who are exploring the other side.

Visit The Other Side NDE YouTube Channel
https://www.youtube.com/@TheOtherSideNDEYT

EIGHT

KATHERINE MASEL

SHE WAS HIT BY A CAR AND WAS SENT TO THE AFTERLIFE; WHAT SHE SAW WILL SHOCK YOU

Katherine Masel shares her profound near-death experience from her childhood. At the age of six, Katherine was hit by a car and found herself floating above her own body, witnessing the aftermath of the accident with heightened awareness. She describes the vivid details of seeing her lifeless form, feeling the emotions of those around her, and encountering a mysterious entity.

Through this remarkable journey, Katherine learned powerful lessons about presence, positivity, and the interconnectedness of all beings. Join us as Katherine recounts this life-changing experience and the insights she gained from it.

Katherine's earliest memories were set against the backdrop of 1960s New Orleans—a city alive with music, festivals, and a cultural tapestry that seemed to hum beneath every interaction. For Katherine, the youngest of eight children, life was a blend of chaotic energy and vibrant color. She could never decide if she loved or loathed being the baby of the family. Some days, it meant endless coddling and playful teasing from her six older brothers; other days, it left her scrambling to be heard in a house that was perpetually buzzing with noise.

Her mother, a resilient woman barely into her forties, was the sun around which the entire household orbited. With eight mouths to feed, she managed the day-to-day demands with an unspoken strength. Katherine was too young to recognize all of her mother's sacrifices, but she sensed in her an unbreakable determination—a quiet refusal to let circumstances define them. Her father worked long shifts at a factory, often returning home late, his clothes smelling of oil and machinery. He wasn't absent, but the burden of emotional and practical care largely fell to Katherine's mother. And then there was Katherine's older sister—more than a decade her senior—

who had taken on a half-mother, half-sibling role. This sister was stern at times and protective at others, a steady presence in a household that rarely paused.

By age six, Katherine was developing a sense of the world around her—an understanding of the unwritten rules that governed her family's lively dynamic. She realized that her mother and sister often exchanged tense, whispered conversations about money, about rent, about rationing the groceries so everyone could have enough. She also watched her six older brothers grow rowdier and more adventurous by the day, their mischief taking ever-new forms in the quiet neighborhoods lining the Mississippi River.

One Monday morning, a hurricane roared in. It wasn't among the legendary storms that would later carve devastation into New Orleans, but it was still fierce enough to knock out power lines, scatter tree branches across lawns, and prompt schools to announce an unexpected closure. For children like Katherine and her siblings, this was a cause for celebration: a free day to roam, to laugh, to be liberated from textbooks and homework. Even the older kids found a certain allure in skipping classes with permission.

Amid the swirling debris and puddles of rainwater, Katherine and one of her middle brothers—Jack—decided to embark on a small adventure. They didn't tell the others; it felt like their little secret. Jack had a bicycle, an old, slightly rusted contraption that he'd rescued from a curb and diligently repaired. Katherine, with her blonde hair still damp from the storm's humidity, perched precariously on the handlebars, squealing with delight each time the bike wobbled or jerked under her brother's steering.

They set off toward the local convenience store to purchase candy—an ordinary, thrilling errand. Their combined coins amounted to a handful of sweets, but they reveled in the idea of tasting sugar on their tongues while the rest of the family was stuck at home. The damp asphalt glistened under a timid sun that had emerged after the storm's retreat. Leaves and branches littered the roadside, giving the city a patchwork of green and brown.

No one saw the speeding car approach. Jack, focused on balancing the weight of his sister on the handlebars, kept his eyes ahead. Katherine leaned back, trusting her brother's every move. Perhaps if they had turned a moment sooner, or if the driver had been more cautious, the accident would have been avoided. But fate had other plans. In a single, heart-stopping instant, everything changed.

The car barreled down the road at a terrifying speed—over 60 miles per hour. The driver, an inexperienced teenage girl, had taken the family vehicle without permission. She was distraught, her knuckles white on the steering wheel. Rounding a bend, she noticed the bicycle too late. She swerved, but there was no time to stop. Jack caught a glimpse of the oncoming danger at the last second, but he couldn't maneuver away in time.

Katherine's world erupted in metallic screeches and sudden weightlessness. She didn't feel the collision, not in the way one might expect. Instead, she was abruptly floating above the scene, her perspective shifted, as though she had been yanked out of her body. All around her, time seemed to slow. Below, she saw her small body splayed on the street, blonde hair stained red with blood. Jack lay nearby, limbs askew, his face contorted in pain and shock.

From this vantage point, she also noticed a young man kneeling beside her broken form. He looked no older than eighteen or nineteen, wearing a T-shirt and jeans. His hands hovered over Katherine's body, trembling with indecision. She could feel his emotions like a wave: confusion, guilt, an overwhelming desire to help but a sense of helplessness in the face of such trauma. He was frantically trying to recall any first-aid training, but his mind was a blank slate, and he was paralyzed by the gravity of the situation.

A few feet away, the car had come to a halt, the front bumper demolished. Steam hissed from the radiator. Standing next to it was the teenage girl driver, tears streaming down her cheeks. She clutched her hair, pacing erratically. Katherine picked up a flood of emotions from the girl—sorrow, panic, and self-condemnation. The girl had taken a reckless risk, and now she might have cost two children their lives. Katherine felt an unexpected surge of sympathy rather than blame. She recognized, even at six, that the girl was simply overwhelmed by guilt, terrified not only of the accident's repercussions but also of her parents' fury.

But Katherine's focus soon shifted, pulled by an even stronger emotional tether. Across the street, she glimpsed her sister. She was usually the calm, collected one, but now she stood ashen-faced, trembling from head to toe. Her eyes were locked on the heap of twisted metal and the small figure sprawled on the pavement. Katherine felt her sister's heart clench with guilt and desperation—an older sibling's sense of responsibility crashing down on her like a tidal wave. "I should have been there," the sister's thoughts seemed to say. "I should have stopped them." There was also a flicker of anger, not truly directed at Katherine but at herself, at circumstances that had spiraled out of control in an instant.

Hovering above this tragic tableau, Katherine sensed no pain, no fear for herself. Instead, she was filled with a profound empathy for everyone involved—Jack, her sister, the driver, the onlookers. She felt simultaneously removed from the chaos, observing it with a strange calm, and intensely connected to each person's emotional state. It was as though she had stepped into a realm where awareness of others' inner lives was completely transparent.

Then came a shift. Behind her, a radiant light manifested. It wasn't a beam like a flashlight or a searchlight; it felt alive, pulsating with a love so pure it took her breath away. Within this light was a being—impossibly comforting, ancient, and deeply familiar. Even though it had no clear face or form, Katherine recognized it on a level that tran- scended logic. The being was offering her a choice, though words weren't spoken. Would she stay in this realm of serene detachment, or return to the life that beckoned her from below?

She hesitated. The serenity here was captivating, free from pain and the weight of earthly existence. But then she thought of her mother. In a flash, she felt her mother's anguish radiating through the crowd, though physically, her mother wasn't yet on the scene. That maternal love was a lifeline, so profound it seemed to span any distance. Before Katherine realized what was happening, her viewpoint changed again. She found herself inside an ambulance, though she wasn't lying on the stretcher. Instead, she was seated beside her mother, who was pleading with paramedics for her daughter's life. Tears streamed down her mother's face, her voice cracking with every word. The ambulance rattled over potholes, lacking the oxygen equipment the paramedics needed. Still, her mother refused to concede, clinging to hope with white-knuckled determination.

In that suspended moment, Katherine understood a depth to her mother's life that she had never seen before. Suddenly, visions of her mother's past filled her awareness. She saw a teenage girl, pregnant in high school, ostracized by her father's family, yet forging ahead with unyielding will. She witnessed her mother's quiet triumphs—finding small jobs to put food on the table, patching up old clothes so her children wouldn't be teased at school, stretching every dollar to ensure they had enough. The images coalesced into a single symbolic vision: a vast field of wildflowers, where one single radiant white bloom stood tall amidst brambles and weeds. That lone flower was her mother—resilient, dignified, refusing to bow to adversity.

Emotion welled up in Katherine. How could she abandon this woman who had fought so hard for all of them? Moved by a surge of love, she cast her gaze back to the luminous being, her choice made: she would return. The being, through a silent understanding, imparted a final message about the power of thoughts and intentions. It was as if a telepathic voice whispered: "What you focus on shapes your reality. Guard your thoughts and direct them toward love."

In the next heartbeat, everything snapped back into place. Katherine was in a hospital room, fluorescent lights glaring overhead. Machines hummed softly. Her head pounded, and the sharp smell of antiseptic stung her nostrils. She blinked, disoriented, realizing she was alive. Though her injuries included a significant gash on her forehead and minor bruises, doctors were stunned that she had survived an impact at such speed with relatively modest damage.

Her family's relief was immeasurable. Her sister, who had been consumed by guilt, cried tears of joy and clutched Katherine's hand. Her brothers visited in shifts, each patting her awkwardly on the shoulder or ruffling her hair, as if they still couldn't quite believe she was okay. Her mother sat vigil, praying silently, occasionally reaching out to rest a hand on Katherine's forearm, as though afraid she might vanish.

In the months and years that followed, Katherine gradually shared fragments of her experience. She spoke of seeing the accident from above, of sensing her sister's turmoil and the driver's fear. One day, she mustered the courage to describe her mother's past visions—the teenage pregnancy, the familial rejection. Her mother's eyes brimmed with tears. No one had told Katherine those details; a six-year-old couldn't have known such things.

For her sister, the greatest shock was Katherine's description of the swirling emotions—guilt, confusion, and even anger—that her sister had felt in that moment of helplessness. Never before had the sister voiced such sentiments aloud, yet Katherine recounted them as though she'd read a private diary. The revelation sparked a moment of healing between them, forging a deeper bond that would fortify their relationship into adulthood.

Over time, Katherine came to see the accident not as a tragedy but as a turning point. The lessons impressed upon her by the radiant being remained an enduring part of her life. She made a conscious effort to guide her thoughts positively, to extend compassion whenever possible, and to cling to hope even in the midst of hardship. Throughout her adolescence, as she encountered typical teenage challenges—insecurities, academic pressures, heartbreak—she often recalled that day. The memory of the light and the love she felt nudged her to make choices aligned with empathy and understanding.

Her mother, too, found solace in Katherine's account. It reaffirmed her belief that love could bridge even the greatest distances, that no matter how dire a crisis, there was a guiding force ready to see them through. And, importantly, it validated that her years of sacrifice had not gone unnoticed, that the quiet battles she fought in her youth had shaped the compassionate mother Katherine so cherished.

As Katherine grew older, stepping into adulthood and eventually motherhood herself, the lessons from her near-death experience continued to influence her decisions. She spoke of it cautiously at first, worried about disbelief or ridicule, but over time, she discovered that sharing her story offered comfort to others in distress. People who heard it gleaned insight into life's interconnectedness and the power of unconditional love.

In fact, more than one friend or relative approached Katherine privately, confessing their own inexplicable brushes with mortality or spiritual glimpses. Her willing-ness to recount her own experience with humility and wonder opened doors for them to speak, to release burdens they had silently carried. In her own gentle way, Katherine became a conduit for healing conversations, reminding everyone that, in times of catastrophe, empathy and love remain our greatest strengths.

Even decades later, if someone were to ask Katherine about that day—the day a speeding car changed her life—she would likely smile with a blend of sadness and gratitude. The accident had undeniably scarred her, but it had also awakened her to a deeper reality: that we each hold the power to transform suffering into wisdom, fear into compassion, and near-tragedy into a testimony of the love that underpins all existence. And though she still bore a thin scar on her forehead as a memento, Katherine considered it less an imperfection and more a reminder of the resilience and love that had pulled her back from the brink.

Ultimately, Katherine's story was never about the accident alone; it was about discovering how hope and love can illuminate even life's darkest corners. From the mother who refused to let her go, to the sister whose guilt was transformed into empathy, to the luminous entity that offered her a choice, every thread in the tapestry of her experience pointed to one simple truth: life, in its fragility, is sustained by the bonds we share and the love we offer one another. And that, more than anything, is what she carried with her—through childhood, adulthood, and into the future, knowing that no storm, no accident, and no fear could ever extinguish the light she found within.

———

NINE
PHILIP HASHEIDER
CLINICALLY DEAD 6 MINUTES; MAN VISITS INFINITE UNIVERSE AND IS SHOWN OUR PURPOSE ON EARTH

On a brisk October morning, Philip Hasheider collapsed in his local hospital's fitness room after finishing a modest set of arm curls, dying for over six minutes. During that time, he found himself in a serene, otherworldly dimension, facing a radiant golden sphere that he sensed was the source of all creation. Bathed in infinite love and witnessing an expanse of countless universes, he felt total peace and acceptance, yet he was drawn back to physical life—where frantic medical personnel succeeded in reviving him. In the months that followed, Philip realized this timing was no coincidence; he'd collapsed precisely where help was at hand because he had a purpose yet to fulfill. Returning with vivid memories of that higher realm, he emerged with a renewed sense of hope, convinced that life here is meant for learning, that love is the universal bond, and that each of us, in our own way, can serve as a conduit of hope for others.

———

On an early October morning, Philip Hasheider discovered an unexpected facet of his own life. The day started like many others on his Wisconsin farm—cool air, faint sunlight breaking through the lingering fog, and the soft lowing of beef cattle in the distance. By 11:00 AM, he would become both an unwitting scholar of dying and, afterward, a determined advocate of hope. He had collapsed on the fitness-room floor at the local hospital, his heart flatlined for more than six minutes, plunging him into a realm beyond human understanding. Yet, just an hour before, he had been alone, trudging quietly through the pasture to check on twenty-seven head of grazing beef cattle.

Throughout that earlier walk, Philip felt an easy calm. The dew on the grass glistened, and a slight breeze carried the scent of harvested crops and hay. Normally, he could

mosey up to the cattle, pat them, and call them by name—
Ginger, Maple, Duke—watching them blink lazily in
approval. But this time, something felt off. About three
hundred feet away, a cow abruptly stood and stared at
him, ears pitched forward, eyes locked. Without warning,
she spun around and galloped, crossing nearly six
hundred feet before pausing to look back. That caused the
entire herd to leap up, forming a collective panic. They
seemed spooked, as if sensing a silent visitor at Philip's
side. It struck him as odd but not alarming. He saw what
he needed—that the animals were generally fine—and
headed back to the house, shrugging off the momentary
oddness.

He had an appointment in a village some twelve miles
distant to get his car's tires replaced. By the time he
climbed into his vehicle, morning had blossomed into a
bright day. Halfway en route, he realized he had time to
spare. Typically, he would have turned right toward the
tire shop, but on a whim, he decided to go left—toward the
local hospital's fitness and rehab center. He parked,
changed into workout clothes, and greeted the five staff
members on duty. They exchanged nods and small talk,
not realizing they were about to witness a turning point in
Philip's life. He ran through a brief stretching routine, then
approached the arm-curl machine, intending a modest set
of twenty reps.

At first, everything felt normal—his arms worked steadily,
engaging each muscle in the controlled movements. But as
he neared the twentieth curl, a peculiar sensation rippled
through both his forearms, as though they were falling

asleep simultaneously. He set down the weights and stood. In a blink, darkness consumed him. One moment, he was in a bright, sterile fitness room—the next, he found himself propelled into a realm beyond mortal comprehension.

He would later struggle for words to describe that space. He felt immersed in a vast "energetic ocean," a field of radiant waves that lapped at him gently, each wave passing through him rather than against him. Glancing down, he observed his form, strangely translucent, each limb and digit outlined by soft luminescence. The sight didn't scare him; on the contrary, he felt tranquil, as though he had simply awakened into a more authentic reality.

In the distance—if distance applied in such a place—he spotted a gargantuan golden-yellow sphere. It glowed with intensity beyond millions of suns, yet paradoxically caused no pain to his eyes. The sphere pulsed, sending out wave after wave of luminous current, each carrying an unmistakable quality of warmth, love, and acceptance. Tiny silver sparks glittered at its surface, darting in random, playful arcs. Philip observed these sparks with awe, sensing that they were a manifestation of pure intelligence, perhaps even the quantum seeds of creation.

It dawned on him that he was beholding what he could only call God—or a "God-essence," an infinite intelligence that formed the core of existence. Tethers, resembling delicate strands or filaments, stretched from the sphere to innumerable universes, anchoring them like pearls on a cosmic thread. Each universe appeared like a thin "sheet of reality," pressed neatly in a vast mosaic of dimensions. Every sheet was linked to the golden sphere, drawing love and life from it, as though the sphere was the heart and the myriad universes its living cells.

Curious, Philip scanned behind himself. Where once he expected to find "empty space," he saw a boundless environment teeming with clarity. The more he peered, the more intricately everything revealed itself, magnifying endlessly. He recognized that all souls, including his own, carried a trace of this God-essence—like luminous shards from a single, eternal gemstone. Time and space felt irrelevant. He was fully at peace, with no sense of fear or longing for his earthly life.

Meanwhile, back in the hospital's fitness room, staff discovered Philip's motionless body. Several paramedics rushed in to commence CPR and set up a defibrillator. Through chest compressions and repeated shocks, they sought to ignite his heart, uncertain if they'd already lost him. None of them could fathom the extraordinary dimension where Philip's consciousness currently roamed. Some called out instructions to one another, their faces etched with urgency. Nurses whispered about the slim chances for revival after so many minutes of cardiac arrest. Yet in that radiant dimension, Philip's awareness floated contentedly, absorbing the God-essence's unconditional acceptance.

Without warning, an abrupt tug yanked him from the cosmic vantage point, hurling him back into his physical body. The abrupt shift felt like being plucked out of calm waters into a whirlwind. When he next gained awareness, hours had passed. He groggily opened his eyes in a hospital bed to find his wife, Mary, massaging his feet, tears in her eyes. His stepchildren hovered, faces pale with concern. The clock displayed 8:00, which mystified him— he swore it should be 8:00 AM, not PM.

Doctors explained he'd been clinically dead for over six minutes, then revived, defying normal medical expectations. Bafflingly, there was no lasting damage to his heart or brain, though the repeated defibrillation and compressions often cause injury. The staff deemed it a miracle. Over the next few days, Philip struggled mentally, grappling with a phenomenon he later labeled "interdimensional confusion." Could a mere six minutes equate to what felt like centuries of experience in that luminous realm? How had he soared through cosmic tapestries, only to return physically intact?

For quite some time, he kept silent about the golden sphere, the countless universes, and his ephemeral, wavelike body. He feared skepticism, dreading disbelief or even ridicule—after all, a farmer claiming an encounter with the infinite was bound to raise eyebrows. Yet a more unsettling question lingered: Why that place, that moment? Had he collapsed earlier, alone among his cows, he might have died unnoticed, hidden in the tall grass. His mind kept circling back to that strange morning, the herd scattering as if fleeing from an unseen force. It wasn't until months later that the pieces finally began to fit together.

Eight months after his near-death, medication complications triggered another collapse. During his recovery, something remarkable happened late one night. Mary witnessed him talking in his sleep, scribbling down his words. He mumbled, "I don't believe it," over and over. When she gently asked what he didn't believe, he muttered: "The reason I came back... to be a conduit of hope for those who have none." When morning came, Mary showed him the note. The words struck him with the weight of revelation. He comprehended that his survival was no accidental fluke but a purposeful event orchestrated by forces beyond his immediate understanding. He returned to this world to serve as a beacon of hope, particularly for those dwelling in despair or disbelief.

Emboldened by that epiphany, he allowed himself to reflect more openly on his cosmic experience. He likened earthly existence to an "off-ramp" from an immense energetic superhighway—our souls voluntarily stepping into this lower vibration dimension for a finite time. Once the "fuel" of mortal life is spent, our true essence returns to the superhighway, traveling to new dimensions or assignments. For him, dying was never meant to be an abrupt end; it was simply a shift in perspective. Unbound by the limits of time and physical form, he had discovered pure love as the very foundation of all existence.

He also realized that his tale carried a message for those burdened by cynicism or overshadowed by the finality of death. There was no question in his mind that a loving intelligence had intervened, ensuring that he collapsed in a hospital fitness room—where staff and the best equipment were available—instead of the remote pasture. The difference between life and death hinged on a single, fateful decision: turning left toward the hospital, not right toward the tire shop. While that might have seemed random at the time, it now resembled divine timing in action.

Philip discovered two key lessons. First was the supreme importance of love, the invisible thread weaving humanity together in everyday acts of kindness and empathy. Second was the ever-present choice of hope, particularly vital in bleak or precarious circumstances. As he communicated these insights, the memory of drifting among cosmic waves and glimpsing a God-essence persisted in his heart. He quietly shared with close friends how the cattle's strange reaction that morning hinted at an aura or sign that only animals could detect, as if they'd sensed death approaching him.

He resumed farm life with renewed wonder, stepping out each day among the livestock, inhaling the crisp Wisconsin air, and cherishing the graceful, routine motion of existence. On the surface, he performed the same chores— feeding hay, monitoring water troughs, scanning for signs of unwell cattle—but inside, he carried the knowledge that there was far more to reality than what his eyes or ears could perceive. The memory of the golden sphere never faded, nor did the recollection of drifting among infinite dimensions, each connected to the source by shimmering threads of love.

From time to time, local community groups or spiritual circles invited him to speak about his near-death experience. Standing before audiences, he'd recount the surreal scene: how he felt the forearms tingle, how in a blink he found himself free of earthly constraints, how entire universes sprawled like pages in a cosmic library, each storyline bound together by a single, radiant light. Some listeners cried, some felt intrigued, and many found renewed faith in the idea that a presence—call it God, call it universal consciousness—held them in unconditional acceptance.

He concluded his talks by asserting that the lessons we glean during and after a brush with mortality can apply to day-to-day living. We need not wait for a crisis to appreciate the gift of existence. We can choose hope, practice kindness, and remain open to the subtle orchestrations that guide our paths. When the final day arrives for any of us, he suggested, we might find it no more terrifying than stepping through a doorway—albeit a doorway to a realm brimming with love and possibility.

Now more than ever, Philip Hasheider stands by his conviction that we all have a role to play in being conduits of hope. As he keeps raising beef cattle, writes his numerous books, or simply sips coffee on a crisp autumn morning, he holds within him the memory of a place beyond measure. If he can do nothing else with his second chance, at least he can impart the simple truth he gleaned from a dimension of pure love: we are connected, always, and the essence of creation is far grander, more patient, and more affectionate than we could ever fathom in ordinary life.

TEN
PHILIP SIRACUSA

14 YEAR OLD DIES AND IS TRANSPORTED TO A HIDDEN REALM BEYOND LIFE; WHAT HE SEES WILL SHOCK YOU

Philip Siracusa shares his profound near-death experience from 1981, which occurred during a routine dental visit in Staten Island, New York. After being administered nitrous oxide, he felt his spirit leave his body, entering a tunnel of light and being transported to what he perceived as Heaven. He describes a beautiful garden, a field of living grass, and an encounter with an angelic being. He also meets his deceased grandparents who tell him it's not his time and send him back to his body. Despite initial skepticism from his family and friends, Philip receives a confirmation of his experience when he and his sister see a girl from Heaven, believed to be their deceased sister, during a walk. This experience profoundly shapes his belief in Heaven and the afterlife, affirming his faith and connection to a higher power.

———

Philip Syracusa was fourteen years old in 1981, an age he spent oscillating between the carefree explorations of childhood and the budding responsibilities of early adolescence. He lived in Staten Island, a place he found both ordinary and enchanting, its borough boundaries a patchwork of suburban neighborhoods and quiet city life. The particular day that changed his life began like countless others: wake up, rush through a quick breakfast, grumble about heading to a dental appointment he'd been dreading for weeks.

In those days, Philip had an uneasy relationship with anything to do with a dentist's chair. The distinctive odor of disinfectant and clove oil, the hiss of the suction tube, the glossy posters of smiling patients—none of it comforted him. Instead, each of these details increased the knot of anxiety in his stomach. But his mother, a petite yet determined woman, insisted he go. A routine check-up and perhaps a filling or two was all it was meant to be. She accompanied him not just out of duty but also out of love, aware of her son's apprehensions.

They arrived at a small, modest practice nestled in one of Staten Island's quieter residential blocks. The office door opened onto a waiting area, its walls lined with outdated magazines and children's reading books. A fish tank bubbled in one corner, providing a soft gurgle that contrasted with the underlying clinical smell. Philip's mother signed him in, then looked over to her son, offering a warm, encouraging smile. Philip returned a timid grin, but the tension in his shoulders never fully eased.

Before long, a nurse summoned them to the examination room. Philip slid into the high-backed chair, carefully adjusting the height for his legs. His mother took a seat in the corner, arms folded, an expression of motherly calm on her face. The dentist, an older man with neatly combed silver hair, entered briskly. His assistant followed, setting trays of gleaming instruments near Philip's chair. The gentle hum of overhead fluorescent lighting and the faint hiss of compressed air filled the space.

Philip tried to steady his nerves, reminding himself that he'd been through this drill (quite literally) before. But as the dentist examined his teeth with a small mirror and probe, Philip flinched under the sharp sensation of metal against sensitive gums. Instinctively, he jerked away, his hand shooting up to grab the dentist's wrist. The dentist pulled back, annoyed. Recognizing Philip's agitation, he turned to his assistant and said something about increasing the dose of nitrous oxide—commonly known back then as "laughing gas," or "sweet air."

Nitrous oxide wasn't a new experience for Philip. He had breathed it in small quantities during past dental procedures, finding that it made him feel slightly giddy and less tense. However, he realized almost immediately that today's dose was different. As the clear plastic mask was set over his nose, the mixture of oxygen and nitrous oxide reached a potency beyond what he'd known. His senses began to swim. A tingling wave swept over his limbs, erasing both fear and pain in an instant.

Then something extraordinary happened: Philip felt his entire body lose weight. He felt suspended, as though gravity had suddenly been deactivated. A hot, spreading sensation, like the onset of powerful anesthesia, surged through his chest. Before he could grasp what was happening, his vision warped. A moment later, he was gazing down at the top of his own head.

It took him a few seconds to comprehend the bizarre perspective. He was floating—not physically, but in some intangible form—above his body. Looking down, he saw the back of the dental chair, the overhead lamp glaring against the metal instruments. He saw his mother, concern etched on her brow, peering at the dentist as he leaned over Philip's prone body. None of them seemed aware that Philip—his consciousness—was now overhead, silently observing.

Strangely, he didn't feel alarm. Instead, there was a curious sense of calm, as though he had stepped outside the realm of normal emotions. A wave of detachment overcame him, and any fear he'd had before vanished. He noted how the dentist bent low, fiddling with instruments, his face set in professional concentration. The assistant hovered near, monitoring vitals or preparing additional tools. Philip's mother watched intensely, her hands clasped, knuckles pale from the tension she was holding in.

No matter how much Philip tried to communicate—willing them to see him, to hear him—they remained fixated on his still physical form. He realized that in this out-of-body state, he could neither speak to them nor affect the physical environment. Then he sensed an irresistible pull coming from above, like a gentle current drawing him upward. He yielded to it, floating effortlessly through the ceiling, leaving the dentist's office and everything in it behind.

In seconds, he found himself no longer in a closed, clinical space but in a vast, swirling tunnel. The sensation resembled being whisked along a river's current, except the water was replaced by luminous energy. He was neither frightened nor overwhelmed; it felt exhilarating. The tunnel contained wind that seemed to roar silently around him, coursing with a magnetism he could only describe as divine purpose. It was as though the wind itself was alive, guiding him toward a distant beacon of light.

As Philip traveled deeper into this vortex, he spotted a pinpoint of brightness up ahead. What started as a tiny speck expanded rapidly until it became a radiant opening. Emerging from the tunnel, Philip felt overwhelmed by an incredible warmth and love radiating from this light. It wasn't harsh like the glare of a stadium floodlight but soft, welcoming, all-encompassing. He stepped into it—though "stepped" might not be the precise term in this weightless reality—and found himself in a realm that stole his breath.

Colors existed here that he couldn't name, surpassing any earthly palette. The sky (or whatever passed for a sky) seemed alive, swirling with ever-shifting hues that pulsed with an undercurrent of joy. Below him, a garden unfurled, breathtaking in its vitality. Each leaf glistened like emerald, each flower boasted a radiance that made it seem lit from within. The very air hummed with gentle harmonies, as though nature itself was singing a perpetual lullaby.

Philip wandered deeper into this garden, each step filling him with awe. He felt more alive than ever before, a clarity of mind and spirit that rendered any earthly feeling dull by comparison. Everything exuded an air of divine perfection. He looked around for any sign of other people—though a moment ago, the idea of "people" seemed irrelevant. Then he sensed a presence approaching from behind.

Turning, Philip saw a young angelic figure—a girl who appeared roughly his age. She had no wings, but her aura glowed with a beauty that transcended human ideals. She radiated kindness and serenity, her eyes reflecting compassion. Without words, she led him to a simple wooden bench near a small, pristine pond. There they sat, and communication flowed telepathically, as though each thought formed was instantly shared. Though no voices exchanged audible words, Philip understood her deeper than he had ever understood anyone.

The angel's presence soothed him. In her mind-thoughts, she reassured him he was safe, that this place was real and that it was connected to a greater reality beyond what humans typically perceive. Philip felt an immense sense of belonging, as though he were returning to a home he hadn't realized he'd left. He basked in the unconditional love emanating from her.

After a timeless interval, the angelic being rose and departed. Almost immediately, Philip noticed two older figures seated on the bench. The moment he saw them, recognition flooded him: they were his paternal grandparents. His grandmother, whom he had known until her passing a few years prior, wore the exact blue dress she had been buried in. His grandfather, in a sharp gray suit and top hat, was someone Philip had heard stories about but never met—he had died well before Philip's birth.

They stood and embraced him, and in that instant, a thousand unspoken affections poured through Philip. It was as though all the emotional disconnects of mortal life evaporated, replaced by a pure bond of familial love. His grandmother smiled, tears of joy in her eyes, remarking telepathically on how much he had grown. His grandfather placed a hand on Philip's shoulder, letting him know how proud he was, even though they'd never met in life. The sensation was indescribably comforting.

But then, almost as quickly as it began, the serenity was overshadowed by urgency. His grandmother's face shifted from delight to concern. She gestured to the horizon, silently conveying that Philip wasn't meant to remain. He wasn't finished with life on Earth. The garden, the angelic realm, all of it began to recede. Philip wanted to stay, so deeply that he felt a pang of sorrow at the thought of leaving. Yet there was an unspoken decree that his time in this realm was temporary—a foretaste, perhaps, of something he would know again when his earthly journey concluded for good.

A force pulled him backward through the tunnel. Colors and warmth faded as the brilliant environment sped away from him, replaced by the blackness of the vortex. The downward journey felt abrupt. In what seemed like a jolt, Philip snapped back into the dentist's chair. The sensation was suffocating, as though squeezing himself into a body that felt too tight. With a gasp, he blinked his eyes, his mother's voice echoing in the background. The bright overhead lamp glared at him, and he tasted the metallic tang of anxiety in his mouth.

Looking around, he saw the startled faces of the dentist, the assistant, and his mother. They were anxious—had he fainted? Overdosed on laughing gas? All he could say, trembling with awe, was, "I've been to Heaven." The dentist dismissed it, chalking it up to a nitrous oxide hallucination. His mother, though concerned, remained uncertain how to respond. She touched his forehead, quietly reassuring him that everything would be okay. Philip, for his part, felt a new calm layered over his teenage nerves. He knew what he had experienced was genuine.

Over the next days and weeks, Philip tried to share the story with friends and family. Some nodded politely, some scoffed, and others shrugged, offering half-hearted explanations involving the effects of sedation. But Philip was steadfast. The memory of that angelic girl, his grandparents, and the breathtaking garden refused to be dismissed as a mere drug-induced dream.

A year later, still haunted by both the dentist's office memory and his own longing for proof, Philip knelt in prayer in his parents' backyard. He begged God for a sign —something tangible that would confirm he hadn't imagined the entire episode. Life continued as usual for a while, and he began to wonder if the sign would come at all. Then, while out walking with his older sister on a mild spring afternoon, Philip saw her: the same angelic girl from Heaven, only now she appeared in everyday clothes —blue jeans and a floral shirt. The sun's rays caught her hair, making it look golden. Stunned, Philip felt his heart pound. His sister saw the girl too. The girl smiled briefly and then disappeared from sight. The encounter lasted mere moments but filled them both with peace and astonishment.

As the years unfolded, Philip pieced together a deeper understanding. He came to believe that the girl might be Linda, a sister who had passed away in infancy before Philip was born. Family lore confirmed that there had indeed been another sibling, lost too soon. This discovery expanded Philip's perspective: the afterlife was no mere theological concept but an actual realm where loved ones, long gone, awaited us. From then on, he spoke of God not as a distant figure but as "a vibration of love, the essence of all creation."

Philip's recollections took on a new significance. What he had seen wasn't just an idyllic snapshot of Heaven; it was a profound reassurance of life's continuity and the interconnected nature of existence. In quiet moments, he still remembered that gentle pull guiding him upward, the vibrant garden, and the unconditional welcome he felt among beings who had transcended earthly limits.

Decades later, Philip's story would become a testament to hope and divine presence. Whenever asked about his out-of-body experience, he recounted details with unwavering clarity: the swirl of colors in the tunnel, the warmth of that indescribable light, the serenity of his angelic companion, and the love radiating from his grandparents. People who heard him recognized the sincerity in his words, the glow in his eyes when he spoke of a place beyond mortal comprehension.

Ultimately, Philip's journey reminded him—and those who listened—that Heaven isn't just a distant idea. It is both a realm of unspeakable beauty and a promise that love never dies. From the vantage point of a teenage boy, overshadowed by a dentist's disapproval and the skepticism of others, the experience transformed into a lifelong mission to share what he learned: that our souls are cherished, that our loved ones remain close, and that we each hold a piece of the divine spark. When he remembered that bench in the garden, he recalled the softness of the breeze and the love that infused everything—and this memory anchored him through life's trials, affirming that no matter how painful or uncertain our earthly existence can be, there is always a place of belonging and peace waiting on the other side.

———

ELEVEN
SCOTT DRUMMOND

CLINICALLY DEAD MAN TRANSPORTED TO ANOTHER REALM; TOLD THE PURPOSE OF LIFE DURING SHOCKING NDE

Scott Drummond shares his incredible near-death experience from 40 years ago. In this heartfelt and compelling account, Scott recounts his journey from a life driven by ambition to an extraordinary encounter with the divine. Learn how this experience transformed his perspective on life, love, and what truly matters. Don't miss this inspiring and thought-provoking story that has touched millions around the world.

Scott Drummond was a man defined by ambitions and the drive to succeed from a young age. Born into a family that eventually fractured in divorce, he learned how to fend for himself quickly. This self-reliance made him keenly aware of the role of finances in shaping opportunity and comfort. Even as a teenager, he set a lofty goal: to accumulate a million dollars by the time he reached 32 so he could retire early and enjoy life without restraint. It seemed a bold aspiration in the late 20th century, but Scott firmly believed it was within his grasp.

He grew up against the backdrop of shifting American life. At 18, he was drafted during the Vietnam era. Unlike many who saw the darkest edges of war, Scott managed to serve primarily on sports teams for the U.S. Army, playing basketball and baseball. These assignments effectively kept him from being sent into the Vietnam conflict. It was a stroke of fortune that both spared him the traumatic horrors of war and allowed him to refine his athletic talents. Afterward, he returned to civilian life and enrolled in college, where his love of sports continued, as did the foundation for his restless ambition.

In the Army, however, he had encountered more than just the avoidance of combat; he found discipline and discovered the thrill of excelling, both in sports and in meeting challenges head-on. This mindset carried over when he eventually left the military. He felt unstoppable, armed with a vision of future success. During his travels, Scott met a remarkable woman in Germany; they married when he was only 21. Reflecting on it later, he would say it was one of the best decisions of his life. His wife became his anchor through an ever-escalating career path that demanded tremendous time on the road.

By 1974, the couple had been married, and over the years, they approached their 50th anniversary—a milestone few achieve. Yet their marital journey wasn't without tension. Scott's corporate aspirations led him to constant travel. Sometimes he was gone three weeks out of every month, leaving precious little time for his wife or for building a stable family life. The rapid career progression—which hinged on stepping over or pushing aside competitors in the scramble for high-paying positions—took its toll on the relationships around him. He had been so set on making money that he sometimes, in his own words, "stepped on a few people." At the time, it didn't matter. The dream of early retirement and wealth overshadowed these moral qualms.

Then came the weekend in December—Scott was 28, home for the Christmas holiday, and he decided to spend a day skiing at Park City, Utah. The air was crisp, the slopes powdered with fresh snow, and the adrenaline of carving down runs at high speed was exhilarating. That evening, Scott took off his gloves and sensed that something wasn't quite right with his hand. Looking down, he discovered, with shock, that his thumb had somehow twisted and was hanging in an unnatural angle, down by his wrist, while his fingers pointed upward. It looked grotesque and impossible to ignore. A friend, an EMT, glanced at it and assured him that no simple band-aid would fix the problem.

Alarmed and in pain, Scott called his wife. She arranged for a surgeon to meet them at a hospital about an hour away. He traveled there, his thumb throbbing, his mind racing with concerns about time off work, potential surgeries, and what it might mean for his career. Throughout the drive, he remained unusually quiet—unaware that his life was about to pivot in ways he couldn't predict.

At the hospital, they prepared him for surgery. He was wheeled into the operating room, garbed in a standard pale-blue gown, fleetingly noticing the stark whiteness of the walls, the overhead fluorescents humming. The tension in the room was subdued but present, an undercurrent that clashed with the standard routine. Scott didn't think to say "I love you" to his wife as he was rolled away—he was too distracted by pain and the swirl of activity. In the back of his mind, he only hoped it would be quick and successful so he could return to chasing his goals.

The anesthesiologist, busy with another crisis, was absent, so the surgeon opted for a Bier block procedure—a common method to numb an entire limb by draining its blood supply, applying an air tourniquet to restrict circulation, and injecting lidocaine. They set up a drape between Scott and the surgical site so he wouldn't see the incisions and sutures. He heard them talking over the partition, exchanging medical jargon and instructions. The procedure, though somewhat unusual to witness, was standard enough in principle.

But as the pressure in his arm increased from the tourniquet, he began feeling significant pain. At the surgeon's direction, a nurse loosened the top valve to relieve some of that pressure. Shortly afterward, when the discomfort rose again, she loosened the second valve—mistakenly failing to first retighten the initial one. In that moment, Scott felt the lidocaine surge past the tourniquet, racing up his arm and crossing his chest. An intense wave of numbness and sedation overwhelmed him. His world blurred.

And then everything changed. One instant he was on the operating table, trapped in a body under local anesthesia; the next, he found himself floating above it, looking down on the small group in the operating room. He saw the surgeon meticulously working on his thumb, the nurse with a panicked expression, and the distinct outline of an EKG machine that abruptly flatlined. The digital beep that signals a heartbeat—stopped. No beep, just a shrill alarm. Scott realized, with eerie calm, that the staff no longer had a heartbeat reading from his body.

He also noticed that an invisible presence stood beside him —an "escort," a being without a corporeal form yet profoundly comforting. This escort seemed neither male nor female. Its calm energy radiated acceptance, as though it was there to guide him. Below, in a blur of frantic motion, the nurse rushed out of the room, visibly distraught, believing she'd killed him. Scott heard her guilt-laden wail. His heart clenched with compassion for her. Even in this disembodied state, he felt empathy. "It's not her fault," he wanted to shout. "Please, don't blame yourself."

The surgeon, meanwhile, didn't immediately realize his patient had flatlined. He continued working on the hand as though in a tunnel-vision focus. Scott's vantage point allowed him to see the skillful incisions, the delicate process of wrapping a tendon around the thumb, all the intricacies that made the body's mechanics so extraordinary. An observer in the corner, the escort nodded in silent admiration. The sudden crisis hadn't changed the doctor's precision.

Then staff members rushed in with defibrillator paddles and other emergency equipment, their voices urgent as they tried to revive him. Scott felt a curious awe. He witnessed every second of their scramble: the frantic bark of instructions, the beeping monitors, the swirl of white gowns. Yet he was also numb to the panic, secure in the presence of the being next to him. Communication between them was telepathic, a gentle understanding. He sensed the escort telling him, *"There is more beyond this."* And in that acceptance, Scott felt neither fear nor regret.

With startling swiftness, the entire scene receded, replaced by a brilliant realm that enveloped Scott's awareness. Suddenly, he was no longer in the operating room but transported to a place of surreal beauty. Tall grass stretched around him in a gently rolling field, the stalks shifting in a mild breeze. Wildflowers of every imaginable hue dotted the area. Each color was more vivid than any he had seen on Earth—purer, as though made of light itself. Above, towering trees rose like living pillars, their branches forming a tapestry of leaves that glowed with radiant health.

Peering upward, Scott saw clouds that were unlike earthly ones. Two of them were bright white on either side of a central cloud tinted with a pearlescent sheen. Rays from these clouds fell onto the field, giving the grass and wild-flowers a gentle shimmer. He felt overwhelmed by a love so profound that it seemed to emanate from every single blade of grass and every petal of each flower. They leaned, almost animate, as if greeting him with an unspoken devotion. This love was deeper than he had ever felt in his life —a love that seemed to acknowledge him intrinsically, an unconditional embrace.

Still accompanied by his escort, Scott stood absorbing the wonder. He noticed that he could see in every direction without turning his head, a panoramic vision that transcended human limitations. The escort told him gently, *"Don't look back,"* as though trying to spare him the temptation of returning to the operating room. Yet, even looking side to side, the color, life, and brilliance around him felt more real than anything he'd ever experienced.

Then, the escort vanished, leaving Scott alone in that field. The solitude didn't frighten him; it felt peaceful. A moment later, as if triggered by an unseen switch, his life began to unfold before him like a meticulously edited film reel. From his earliest infancy to the present at age 28, he watched events replay with stunning clarity—moments he'd forgotten or never realized held such significance. He saw his parents, remembered the strain of divorce, re-experienced the proud and tender times with them. He revisited his teenage years, the naive bravado of enlisting in the Army, and those exhilarating times on the basketball and baseball courts. He watched his younger self rush toward success, sometimes neglecting or pushing away those who loved him.

In this life review, he didn't just see events; he felt them. Every expression of kindness or cruelty he had shown radiated back to him. He felt the joy of small acts of service, the sting of a harsh word. None of his prized possessions—boats, fancy homes, lavish vehicles—mattered. What shone through was how he treated people, how his actions impacted their emotional well-being. His corporate achievements, the houses and material upgrades, faded into irrelevance. All that counted was the love or the harm he had given. And even the painful realizations were delivered with profound love, as though the universe itself was showing him truths without condemnation.

Once the review ended, a sense of calm replaced the flurry of emotions. Scott recalled looking up at the central pearl-tinted cloud. He heard a simple command: "Come." The flowers, the grass, and rays of light seemed to guide him forward, beckoning him to cross that final distance. Reaching the cloud, he saw an arm extend, impossibly strong, large, and imbued with an indescribable affection. This arm offered him a hand, an invitation to grasp it fully. In that moment, he understood that he was indeed deceased, that crossing this threshold meant he wouldn't return to Earth. The arm's presence flooded him with a love so overwhelming that he yearned to hold on forever.

But as he lifted his own hand to seize that promise of eternal rest, the arm withdrew, slipping back into the cloud. Twice, Scott tried to grasp it, craving that love, that acceptance. A voice—deep, certain, and full of compassion —rang out: *"It is not yet your time. You have more things yet to do."* That instruction echoed in his mind like a fateful chord, filling him with equal parts disappointment and awe. Suddenly, the brilliance vanished. He found himself hurtling back into his physical form.

He awoke to a shock: medics and hospital staff were wheeling him out of the operating room, a sheet pulled over his body. A certificate on his chest read that he'd been dead for twenty minutes. Gathering his strength, Scott forcefully flipped off the sheet, startling the doctor and nurses who believed they were transporting a corpse. They scrambled to reassure his wife that he was alive, though no one—least of all the frantic staff—had realized what had actually transpired during those 20 minutes of clinical death.

The days that followed were surreal. Though his thumb was bandaged and healing, his perspective on life had changed irrevocably. Colors seemed brighter, more intense. His sense of empathy soared. He discovered he had a peculiar gift of "tasting" colors, an odd synesthetic ability that was simultaneously wondrous and mystifying. For three days, an extraordinary peace enveloped him, a peace that made normal life feel jarringly mundane. He told the doctor about his inner turmoil—how a part of him fought to stay in that place of love, even as his body pulled him back to living. The doctor was baffled.

Scott tried sharing his story with friends and family. Some dismissed it as a product of anesthesia or an overactive imagination. Feeling wounded by skepticism, he closed up, treasuring the experience as sacred. The memory lingered, unspoken, for a long time.

Years later, a reporter inquired about near-death experiences, but Scott wasn't yet ready to dissect it publicly. The memory was too personal, too reverent. Eventually, about three years ago, at the urging of a close friend who hosted a podcast, he retold the entire story. He thought it would be a niche interest—just another tale amid countless YouTube testimonies. Instead, it went viral, amassing millions of views as strangers from around the world resonated with his honesty and detail.

Now in his 70s, Scott regards that event as a spiritual turning point. He sees his younger self, the relentless pursuit of wealth, and all the times he overlooked family and compassion, and realizes how inconsequential material things become when weighed against genuine human connection. Money can make life comfortable, but it can never replicate the unearthly love he felt in that radiant field, nor replace the importance of how we treat one another.

In reflecting on it all—his Army days, his corporate climb, his near-death, and his unexpected platform as a voice for spiritual experiences—Scott Drummond says the same message he's been saying for decades: "It's not just about the money and the achievements. It's about the heart. It's about showing kindness, building people up, offering love when we can, and knowing that in the end, all that truly matters is how we've loved and been loved in return."

———

TWELVE
ULLA GAUDIN

CLINICALLY DEAD FOR 20 MINUTES;
WOMAN CROSSES OVER AND IS SHOWN
THE TRUTH ABOUT EARTH

In her early twenties, Ulla Gaudin was trapped in an abusive relationship and struggled with an advanced cancer diagnosis in Finland. One night, after enduring a brutal beating by her boyfriend, she effectively died on the hospital bed, finding her consciousness outside of her body and gazing down at the frantic medical efforts. Surrounded by light and greeted by her long-deceased grandparents, she experienced a heightened sense of perception, feeling love radiating from every living element—even the winter trees outside. Offered a choice to remain in this transcendent realm or return to physical life, she chose to come back, convinced she still had a purpose. She awoke to discover that her cancer had vanished, astonishing her doctors, and she ultimately escaped her abuser. Today, she believes wholeheartedly in our ability to reshape reality through love and openness, viewing death not as an end but as a passage to a higher expression of who we truly are.

Ulla Gaudin was originally from Finland, where she spent much of her youth. Her upbringing fostered a deep admiration for the stark beauty of Nordic winters, the rolling green of the brief summers, and a culture rich in quiet resilience. Yet, beneath that surface of normalcy, she carried a private burden: an abusive relationship that began when she was just sixteen. This young man—at first the only one who ever professed love for her—eventually became a perpetrator of violence, trapping her in a cycle of trauma from which she found no easy escape.

Over the years, the abuse escalated, culminating in repeated physical assaults. Though she was outwardly stoic, internally her spirit was fraying. By the time she reached twenty-one, she received devastating news: she had developed stomach cancer and doctors grimly predicted she would live no more than two years. It baffled her to be so ill at such a young age, but the stress and brutality of her circumstances provided a possible explanation, as unrelenting trauma can undermine the body's resilience.

Still, her cancer was not what finally ended her life on that harrowing night—it was her boyfriend's violence. He had a habit of heavy drinking, staying out late with his circle of friends. More than once, he returned home inebriated, directing anger and aggression toward her. One particular night—an otherwise uneventful evening that she hoped might pass without incident—turned catastrophic. Deep asleep, she was startled awake by the sound of him stumbling in. In a terrifying instant, he was on top of her, rousing her with vicious blows aimed at her abdomen. Strikes to the stomach do not leave easily visible bruises on the outside, so he routinely attacked her there, a cruel tactic that allowed his assaults to remain hidden from neighbors or authorities.

This night, his demeanor was more unnerving than ever, a dark malice flickering in his eyes. She recalled his hands gripping her neck, choking her while he bit at her eyebrow, cutting her skin with his teeth. After that, consciousness slipped away, and the next thing she knew she was in a chaotic hospital setting, medical staff crowding around.

In a moment of surreal detachment, she watched doctors shouting orders and saw tubes and machines—all presumably for a patient in crisis. Slowly, she realized that patient was her, sprawled on the hospital bed, lifeless. Initially, panic tried to grip her, but as soon as it surfaced, the feeling evaporated, as though someone or something lifted it from her. She felt herself hover slightly off the ground, noticing that she was not simply at a vantage point near the ceiling. Instead, she was anchored in an odd in-between, about nine feet high along a back wall. She saw her own battered body below, surrounded by frantic healthcare personnel attempting to revive her.

An immediate sense of peace overtook her—an extraordinary calm, quite removed from the horrifying violence that had placed her here. Astonishingly, nothing about this vantage felt unnatural. From this perspective, she became aware that she was no longer in a physical body but rather in a state of pure awareness. The world of hospital floors and medical staff had a muted, dreamlike quality, while her vantage point felt vividly real.

Curious, she checked her arms—only to discover she had no arms in the usual sense. How could she still see? She did not seem to possess eyes or a head as people do, yet visual information was undeniably pouring in from all angles. Her consciousness encompassed the entire space, allowing her to observe doctors, nurses, hospital corridors, and even the wintry scene outside the building. The brilliance of colors shocked her: the bleak midwinter sky and tree branches, supposedly barren or frosted, now pulsed with an uncanny luminosity. She felt the life force of those trees—even though, physically, they were locked in the freeze of a Finnish winter.

Then, she sensed two presences approaching. Her paternal grandparents, who had been deceased for more than a decade, stood close by—though not in typical human form. They appeared as grand, radiant beings, almost shapeless but unmistakably them. She perceived their personalities and love as strongly as if they wore name tags. Even though they had long since passed, here they emanated a vibrancy and warmth that dwarf anything from their mortal years. She heard no voices in the conventional sense, but knew what they communicated: deep love, relief at seeing her, and a shared recognition of her predicament.

She became aware of others, too—perhaps extended family or ancestral spirits—forming a supportive presence. Yet, she primarily conversed with her grandparents, discovering they could simultaneously be "in several places at once." They gently radiated acceptance, explaining that she now stood in a boundary state between earthly life and whatever lay beyond. Their loving energy enveloped her, dislodging any fear of what had just happened to her body. This perspective was so serene that, for a moment, she nearly forgot the trauma that brought her to this junction.

Peering through walls and ceilings, she realized how easily she could shift her focus. She looked outside, appreciating the mesmerizing synergy of colored auras enveloping the trees, bushes, and even the stark hospital façade. The world sparkled with a heightened clarity, the dullness of everyday perception replaced by effervescent life. The staff, frantically working on her physical form, were overshadowed by her grandparents' calm assurance that everything was under control. She briefly noted the doctors' frustration—her heart refused to beat—and overheard them preparing to call the time of death.

It was at that point that her grandparents offered her a choice: stay in this elevated state, joining them more fully in the afterlife, or return to her physical existence. Strangely enough, both options carried no condemnation, no heavy moral burden. They impressed upon her that free will reigned in such instances. She recognized how battered she was from months of violence and the exhaustion of fighting stage-four stomach cancer. On the other hand, she felt an equally urgent pull back to Earth—she had responsibilities, she had an inner calling yet unmet, and a sense that her story there was unfinished.

With the entire cosmic vantage swirling around her, she chose to return. At that moment, time ceased to be an abstract flow. She watched her grandparents recede, still smiling, still emanating unconditional support. In a thunderous jolt, a fierce wave of pain overwhelmed her as she slammed back into her body. The shocking weight of limbs, the heartbeat's pulse, the stings of battered flesh, and the oxygen entering her lungs all roared into her awareness. Opening her eyes, she saw the hospital staff exclaiming that her heart had spontaneously revived— doctors reevaluated the situation, frenetically adjusting their predictions. By all rights, she should not have made it.

Still battered, she faced a unique dilemma: she felt entirely healed on a spiritual level. The cancer, which had threatened her life for years, was effectively gone. Doctors, who had tested her again and again, discovered the malignant cells had vanished—an impossible scenario unless some extraordinary healing event had intervened. They insisted she remain hospitalized for observation, convinced that her revived heart might fail again or that the cancer had only gone into hiding. But subsequent tests confirmed: no cancer remained. Confounding the medical professionals, she stood at the edge of an enigma—why had her cancer vanished so abruptly?

She returned home to a precarious situation with her abusive boyfriend, who had put her in the hospital in the first place. Yet, ironically, her perspective had undergone such a radical shift that initial fear of him was, in part, supplanted by a deeper awareness of her own power to craft a new path. She realized how precarious it was to remain with him, but also recognized the freedom inherent in her capacity to alter reality. If she could step beyond the illusions that had enslaved her to fear, perhaps she could orchestrate a life free from violence.

The first year after her NDE was turbulent. Despite her new convictions, she felt hyper-sensitive to energies around her. She sensed the emotional states of trees, animals, or strangers passing by—an overwhelming sensitivity that threatened to drown her in stimuli. She discovered she needed to develop an "energetic shield," learning to safeguard herself from absorbing the pain of others, which at times felt crippling. Occasionally, she lapsed into moments of regret, fleetingly wishing she had not returned, especially when confronting difficulties left behind in the physical world. But the memory of her grandparents, their radiant love, and the vast acceptance on the other side, reminded her that she had specifically chosen to come back.

Bit by bit, her life's tapestry wove anew. She summoned the courage to leave her abuser for good. The once fatal cancer now nothing more than a file in medical records. Despite doctors proclaiming she'd never conceive children, she eventually bore two. Each day felt like an invitation to re-create her world, reaffirming the fundamental insight gleaned from her near-death: our beliefs and emotional orientation hold astonishing power in shaping our experiences. She taught herself, then others, how to harness that capacity.

Some of her revelations included the sense that death is not a final end but a movement to a higher expression of ourselves. She told friends that "heaven and hell" might be more subjective states of being than physical locales, emphasizing that once freed from bodily constraints, souls remain curious about earthly happenings, attuned to the loved ones still incarnate. For her, the afterlife was not a distant heaven but a dimension lying just beyond the bandwidth of ordinary perception. She discovered it was a place of shimmering color, fluid time, and unconditional acceptance.

Now, decades later, Ulla Gaudin looks upon her life with a calm gratitude. Where once she had been a victim—both of cancer and domestic brutality—she evolved into a living testament to resilience and transformation. She cherishes her children, in whom she sees the embodiment of free will and the power to shape reality. As she embraces each new dawn, the memory of standing among swirling colors and feeling the unconditional love of her deceased grandparents resurfaces, fueling her mission to help others, especially women, break free from trauma.

She occasionally addresses gatherings or supports individuals grappling with PTSD. She conveys her own experiences not as mere anecdote but as a living example of how each of us wields the power to reimagine our reality. Yes, she admits, it might take more than 24 hours for most people to cure themselves of dire illnesses or extricate themselves from impossible situations, but she contends the principle is the same: we are far more creative, far more potent, than our ordinary lives betray. At her side, or just behind her shoulder, she senses the presence of her grandparents, that tranquil vantage point in the hospital, and the endless matrix of love she glimpsed beyond mortal life.

And so she persists, forging forward with the clarity that life is endless. Our ephemeral human adventures might end, but the spirit carries on—whether guiding, learning, or reuniting with dear ones left behind. For her, acknowledging the illusions of limitation in this world permits the magic of creation to surge forth. She can now take that knowledge into late-night calls with women who fear for their safety, or those battered by misfortune, offering not mere words but an authenticity forged from her own crossing into and back from death's threshold. Her very presence radiates the conviction that no matter how bleak circumstances appear, love can—and will—break through, if we only remember the infinite scope of our being.

———

THIRTEEN
VICKI WERNER
WOMAN IS TRANSPORTED TO ANOTHER REALM WHERE SHE IS SHOWN THE SOUL'S PURPOSE

Vicki Werner recounts her near-death experience in 2012 after a traumatic past. Her journey involves seeing her family and loved ones on the other side, being shown their lives without her, and being offered three gifts before choosing to return to her body.

In 2012, Vicki Warner's heart stopped for eight full minutes. Doctors would later call her survival a miracle, but for Vicki, it was far more than that: it was a personal journey that began long before her body shut down and ended only when she chose to fight her way back to life. As she would tell it, the seeds of her near-death experience were planted in 2004, when she and her husband underwent a grim and life-altering trauma—an event so harrowing that it fractured the careful balance of Vicki's psyche.

She was no stranger to ordinary challenges. Raised in a tightly knit family, she learned early the value of self-reliance. Yet nothing in her upbringing prepared her for the complexity of severe Post-Traumatic Stress Disorder (PTSD). In those first months following the trauma, she assumed she'd heal over time, as people often claim injuries do. But the reality was a harsh reminder that emotional wounds can't always be erased by the simple passage of days or weeks. PTSD, in her experience, didn't fade; it continued to intensify, pushing her nervous system into a perpetual state of alarm.

By 2012, Vicki recognized the extent of her body's rebellion. Joint pain assaulted her daily, leaving her stiff and aching upon waking. Chronic fatigue drained her energy even though she tried to rest whenever possible. Frequent waves of nausea sapped her appetite, leaving an unceasing sense of queasiness. In truth, she felt as though her body were gradually shutting down, battered by long-term stress no one could fully comprehend. She and her husband searched far and wide for a solution—visiting specialists, exploring unconventional therapies, seeking respite wherever it might be found.

November of that year found Vicki and her husband traveling once more, but this time not for her own healing; she planned to assist her sister during childbirth. Having trained informally as a doula, Vicki knew how to apply counter pressure to ease her sister's pain. She worked carefully, pressing certain points in her sister's back, focusing on the growing surges of labor. But in the midst of what should have been a profound, family-centered moment, Vicki sensed something amiss. A wave of weakness tore through her, and her life force seemed to vanish from her fingertips. She collapsed, her sister calling her name, but her consciousness hovered on the brink of complete disengagement. Although the haze lifted just enough for her to realize that her sister needed her, Vicki couldn't shake the feeling that something was very wrong.

Two weeks later, back home and still feeling drained, Vicki decided on a whim to bolster her stamina with a liquid B12 supplement. She had purchased it from a local herb store, intending only a quarter teaspoon—a standard dosage. Distracted, she accidentally poured a quarter cup instead, an amount easily 20 times the recommended measure. The moment the liquid passed her lips, she was struck by intense heat and crippling pain. Realizing her mistake, she acted swiftly, forcing herself to vomit, praying it would expel the excess. Yet the pain endured, and violent muscle spasms seized her frame, accompanied by uncontrollable trembling. Panicked and unsure what else to do, she managed to contact her husband, who rushed her to the emergency room.

In the ER, Vicki's condition perplexed the medical staff. She moaned in agony, her body twisting with each muscle spasm. After minimal observation, a flurry of tests, and a short evaluation, a doctor diagnosed her with gastritis—an inflammation of the stomach lining—and discharged her. Vicki walked out in a daze, uncertain, still racked with pain. The next day, that precarious sense of unwellness spiked to a breaking point as she lay alone in bed. Her limbs felt robbed of all strength, and her breathing grew shallow. A strange luminescence filled the bedroom, almost like a gentle halo of light. She sensed a tug deep in her core, an eerie magnetism drawing her away from her physical form.

Before she could comprehend what was happening, she found herself at the foot of the bed, gazing upon her weakened body. It lay on the mattress, small and fragile under the bedcovers. Instead of the horror one might expect, Vicki felt a profound wave of compassion for that suffering figure. It dawned on her that she was somehow outside herself, no longer tethered to flesh and bone. Glancing at the clock, she noted the time was 6:52 PM, December 16, 2012. Yet the precision of this detail felt strangely immaterial in the face of so extraordinary an occurrence.

A moment later, she wasn't in the bedroom at all. She was in the living room, gazing upon her family: her husband and daughters seated around the television. They were watching The Simpsons, and she recognized her husband's distinctive laughter echoing through the house. Bemusement flickered in her: even in this out-of-body state, she felt a pang of annoyance that The Simpsons might be too adult for her young girls. But that was overshadowed by a deeper emotion—love so vast that it nearly brought her to tears. She longed to plop down onto the floor with them, to join their comfortable routine, but she understood she physically could not.

Without warning, she and her family shifted to an unfamiliar place. A wide pathway stretched before them, and her loved ones stood at the top—her husband holding their youngest daughter, Sophie, and her older children gathered around. One by one, each expressed they would ultimately be fine if she had to leave them. Tears lined her husband's face as he declared, "I'll be okay," choking back the heartbreak implied. Her children echoed the sentiment, each in their unique, plaintive way. She sensed extended family and friends further behind them, silent supporters, all gently insisting they'd manage if she passed on. This did not feel like a dream or some half-baked hallucination; it was heartbreakingly real—an orchestrated farewell, if she chose to cross over.

Then, as though tugged by an invisible cord, Vicki was whisked away. Her loved ones' figures receded, and she found herself approaching a looming structure—an eerie, run-down building reminiscent of a haunted mansion. A rational part of her expected fear, yet curiosity overshadowed any dread. The building's decaying exterior and crooked shutters stood as silent sentinels of decay, but inside, everything changed in the blink of an eye. The dingy walls morphed into a magnificent golden dome, awash in life and brilliant, pulsing colors. It exuded warmth and vibrancy that transcended anything terrestrial. Every atom in this place felt saturated with love.

At the center of the dome, three radiant beings awaited her arrival. Their forms glowed with a comforting light, not blinding but enveloping. Communicating telepathically, they explained that her body was in critical condition—ravaged by severe illness and the cumulative impact of her trauma. Her soul, they told her, had entered a transitional phase. The building's haunting facade was a symbol of the emotional decay she bore, while the luminous interior revealed the promise of healing if she chose to continue forward.

Yet these guardians also showed her a series of visions about her family's future if she decided to stay in this realm, never returning to life. She saw her husband's descent into solitude and her children struggling emotionally without her. Each scene broke her heart, but one revelation struck with particular force: her youngest daughter, Sophie, would never fulfill her life's purpose if Vicki did not return to raise her. Something about Sophie's destiny hinged on her mother's presence. That knowledge settled within her, bringing a surge of maternal determination.

She looked at the three beings with newfound resolve. "I have to go back," she declared telepathically. There was no hesitation in their acceptance, no argument against her choice. In a flash of brilliant light, the golden dome vanished. Vicki found herself catapulted back into her bed, reeling from a severe, throbbing ache in her entire body. Slowly, painfully, she forced herself upright, tears of both agony and a strange relief rolling down her cheeks.

Not long afterward, her husband and children entered to say their nightly prayers. Sophie, her youngest, crawled onto the bed. Though Vicki's voice was spent from exhaustion, Sophie leaned in and whispered, "I need you, Mommy." That moment mirrored what Vicki had seen in the dome: the child's life thread tightly bound to her mother's presence. Vicki let tears answer the plea she couldn't vocalize. She silently promised she wouldn't leave her daughter behind.

The months that followed were some of the hardest in Vicki's life. Her entire body felt as though it were in open revolt—organs fragile, her mind weighed by exhaustion. Eight months passed in which she scarcely left her bed, every day a battle to replenish her strength. But intertwined with this relentless struggle was a steadfast commitment to the living. She had chosen to return, and in that choice, she clung to the resolution to heal, no matter how long it took.

Bit by bit, she made progress. Gentle stretches evolved into short walks, which eventually allowed her to stand for longer periods. She adopted a regimented approach to diet, rest, and meditation, taking to heart the idea of re-regulating her nervous system. She also nurtured the emotional side of her recovery—regularly revisiting the memory of her out-of-body experience, recalling the golden dome and the comforting presence of those luminous beings. She recognized that profound healing required addressing not merely her physical state but the underlying trauma and sorrow that had permeated her life for years.

Though no single epiphany erased her PTSD overnight, the near-death experience provided a spark of hope and direction. She sought therapy catered to trauma, engaged in stress-management techniques, and communicated more openly with her family about her needs, her limitations, and her heartfelt wish for deeper bonds. Her husband—once a silent bystander to her internal battles—grew more empathetic, acknowledging that his wife had journeyed through something beyond comprehension.

Vicki also found a quiet solace in spiritual practices she had once dismissed. She lit candles, prayed, journaled, or simply listened to calming music, all the while casting her mind back to the golden dome and the gentle reassurance of the three beings. She recalled how they had shown her that the battered, haunted structure symbolized her own battered psyche—yet even something so apparently ruined could open to brilliance and love within.

As years passed, her story began to spread among close friends and family, some of whom asked her to speak about it at informal gatherings or prayer circles. She found that narrating the experience was like unlocking the lessons she'd been given. Each retelling reminded her of the reasons she'd chosen to fight to survive: love for her children, a desire to guide them, and the knowledge that all the pain in her life hadn't wiped out her inherent purpose.

Crucially, she realized that PTSD's hold on her was loosening. The nightmares that once interrupted her sleep diminished in frequency. She grew better at identifying and interrupting stress triggers, summoning the memory of the dome whenever she felt the familiar cold hand of anxiety grip her chest. Though she would never forget the trauma that had begun her decline in 2004, she no longer saw it as a permanent condemnation but rather as a chapter in a larger story—one that featured redemption, fortitude, and resilience.

By the time Vicki neared full recovery, she had gained an intimate perspective on life's fragility. The eight minutes she spent clinically dead might have seemed brief in objective time, but in her consciousness, they spanned endless emotional landscapes. She recognized the ephemeral nature of existence, tempered by the profound ties of love. Rather than mourning the illusions of safety she'd once held, she embraced the knowledge that every moment with her family was precious, a gift she'd once nearly forfeited.

She spoke openly about her experiences with others going through serious illness, hoping to inspire them to cling to hope. She'd remind them that even when the body seems to fail and despair grows strong, there can be a chance to rediscover meaning and reclaim life. To those traumatized by events in their past, she would gently say that trauma need not dictate an entire lifetime. Healing, slow as it might be, remains possible—and sometimes, extraordinary moments can light the way.

In reflecting on her near-death experience, Vicki recognized that while doctors might view her survival simply as a puzzle of biology, she perceived it as an affirmation of the hidden interplay between life, love, and grace. She never discounted medical science for saving her life—after all, it was the doctors' initial interventions that kept her body stable long enough for her to choose. But the deeper layers, the realm of the golden dome and the luminous guardians, convinced her that human life is guided by forces beyond mere physical processes.

Sometimes people asked if she feared dying again. To this, Vicki's answer was subtle and calm: no, she did not. That didn't mean she courted death, only that she had glimpsed what lay beyond it and found it neither terrifying nor lonely but suffused with abiding love. She would hold her children close, remembering how nearly she had lost the chance to see them grow, and her heart would surge with gratitude.

Ultimately, Vicki Warner's story is one of delicate balance: the slow unraveling caused by a devastating trauma, the near-disintegration of her body from untreated distress, and then the miraculous pivot during an 8-minute brush with death that compelled her to rediscover the value in living. From the entire ordeal, she retained a fierce belief in the resilience of the human spirit. And whenever she felt her mind waver, threatened by doubts or the sting of old memories, she'd close her eyes and envision a tattered mansion turning into a radiant temple, golden light flooding her vision, a reminder that even in the ruins of heartbreak, there can be a door leading to wonder and hope.

———

FOURTEEN
VINNY TOLMAN
HE DIED AND WAS SHOWN WHY WE
EXIST AND EARTH'S PURPOSE

In 2003 Vinney Tolman experienced a breath-taking near-death experience after he and a friend decided to experiment with a new supplement while bodybuilding.

During his NDE, Vinney doesn't meet God or Jesus or a family member like most people. Instead, he is met by a man he's never met before but will be introduced to in the upcoming months following his NDE.

———

Vinnie Tolman did not consider himself the type of person who flirted with mortality. At the start of 2003, he was deeply invested in personal health, an amateur body-builder who meticulously balanced his workouts with careful dietary choices. He also worked as a home builder, a trade he considered both physically challenging and creatively fulfilling. On top of that, he had a side involve-ment in television and film, proof of his restless nature—always on the lookout for new opportunities. If ever asked about the main focus in his life, he would have pointed to his physical wellbeing. He had learned early on that caring for one's body, fueling it with the right supplements, and maintaining a rigorous exercise schedule were corner-stones for success.

But in a single, fateful moment, everything changed. Vinnie and a close friend had just begun testing out a new nutritional supplement. Their initial doses prompted an uneasy feeling in both of them; neither felt quite right. The day took a turn when they decided to grab a quick bite at a fast-food restaurant. Upon entering, Vinnie's friend slumped into the first available booth, overcome by dizzi-ness, while Vinnie went to the restroom, locking the door behind him. The last conscious recollection he had was slipping and tumbling onto the tile floor—and a sudden wave of intense nausea. As darkness pulled at the edges of his mind, he began to vomit while lying on his back, inadvertently choking and slipping away into death.

Simultaneously, in the main dining area, his friend also lost consciousness. He sprawled across the booth, vomiting profusely, which drew immediate concern from the restaurant's manager. Alarmed by the distressing scene, the manager phoned emergency services. Paramedics arrived in a whirlwind of noise and urgency, quickly assessing Vinnie's friend. They whisked him into an ambulance and sped off to the hospital, where he would be treated and discharged the following day, battered but alive.

Tragically, no one realized that Vinnie was dying or, more precisely, already dead behind the locked restroom door. In a surreal merging of time and space, Vinnie found himself floating in a vantage point outside normal reality. It felt strangely serene, as though nestled in a soft, weightless cocoon. From that vantage, he saw a vivid scene unfold below him: the manager and staff huddled around his friend, the bustle of incoming paramedics hauling him away. But nobody even glanced toward the restroom. For a while, Vinnie did not comprehend that the lifeless body on the floor—a form contorted on cold tiles—belonged to him. He observed it with a curious detachment, the features contorted and the complexion oddly different from his usual healthy glow.

A moment later, a restaurant patron approached the locked restroom, tried the handle, and discovered it wouldn't budge. Concerned, the patron forced the door open, encountering the shocking sight of Vinnie's motionless figure. Urgently, they contacted emergency services again, this time for Vinnie. Medical operators guided them over the phone on basic steps until paramedics could return. By the time a second ambulance arrived, the paramedics found no pulse, no breathing. An official pronouncement of death was made.

Amidst the commotion, a rookie medic was ordered to fetch a body bag. He diligently retrieved one and placed Vinnie's corpse inside it, zipping it shut. Then, left to handle the grim task, the rookie sealed the bag and resumed standard protocol. As the ambulance drove away, presumably heading to the morgue or a hospital's holding area, Vinnie's consciousness witnessed all of it from a dimension beyond. He heard the radio chatter, sensed the electric tension, and, most strikingly, perceived the rookies' thoughts—a swirl of reluctance and heartbreak. The rookie felt that something was amiss. Vinnie noticed a faint glow radiating from the man's chest—a sign of compassion, perhaps, or a silent calling to challenge the official pronouncement.

Suddenly, a thunderous voice seemed to speak words that transcended the physical plane: "This one's not dead." As if guided by an unseen presence, the rookie paused, dismissed the earlier instructions, and decided to check again for any signs of life. He unzipped the body bag and tried to detect a pulse. Finding none at the usual spots, he moved to Vinnie's femoral artery, pressing near his thigh bone. The moment he made contact, Vinnie felt a searing jolt, even in his disembodied state. It was as though a conduit had opened between his essence and his inert flesh.

Ignoring the admonitions of more experienced paramedics, the rookie proceeded with resuscitation. He hooked up a defibrillator, ignoring voices scolding him that it was already too late. The rookie remained determined, guided by what he sensed to be a second chance. The first two charges yielded no results, but on the third, the EKG monitor erupted into a frantic beep. Vinnie suddenly had a heartbeat. The ambulance roared to life with renewed urgency, sirens blaring to get him to the hospital.

During the rush, as medical staff transferred Vinnie into a hospital trauma bay, his body convulsed in seizures. Now, from this disembodied perspective, he felt everything— every strap tightened around his limbs, every injection, every barked command from the doctors attempting to keep him alive. A wave of fear cascaded through him. Dark memories flickered at the edges of his awareness, overshadowing the miracle of being revived. But in that chaos, a comforting warmth materialized. It was as if a door had opened in his mind, letting in rays of love and serenity.

He found himself in a place devoid of chaos, at once silent and radiant. Before him stood a calm figure: a man dressed in a simple white garment, emanating a glow that spoke of kindness and wisdom. Their eyes met, and Vinnie realized this being was neither God nor Jesus but something akin to an assigned guide. The man's name, conveyed telepathically, was Drake. Drake's eyes shone with unwavering love, as though everything Vinnie ever did or would do was accepted without condition.

Confusion washed over him. He could recall fleeting images of the ambulance, the paramedics, the shock of electrical paddles. Then there was Drake, explaining that Vinnie existed in a state of transition. This place, a threshold between life and what people often call "the Other Side," was not frightening but brimming with compassionate presence. Drake's role, he explained, was to guide Vinnie "wherever he wanted to go," be it further into the realms of spirit or back to the physical world he had just departed.

In an unfolding series of revelations, Drake led Vinnie on a journey filled with lessons and glimpses of profound truth. They discussed authenticity—how wearing masks in life diminishes the soul and hinders connection. Drake elaborated that Earth is akin to a grand school, where each lifetime presents opportunities to grow in empathy, resilience, and the capacity to love. Vinnie felt compelled by these revelations: The small everyday acts of kindness and genuine interactions with others hold deeper meaning than we realize.

As they ventured further, Vinnie noticed that everything in this realm appeared alive from within. The grass, if that was the right word for it, glowed with an internal luminescence. Flowers, swaying softly, seemed sentient, radiating an acceptance that Vinnie found utterly disarming. Even the trees, reminiscent of those in grand, ancient forests, shimmered with an internal energy that all but sang with divine consciousness. Birds—or their equivalent—passed overhead in arcs of soft, colorful light. Drake encouraged him to experience the harmony saturating this environment: a peace more all-encompassing than anything Vinnie had sensed in his earthly life.

In the distance, a majestic building rose into view—a structure that had the aura of an ancient university. Its arches and columns glimmered with an intrinsic light, a testament to the wisdom housed within. Vinnie felt drawn to its broad steps, sensing it was a place of ongoing learning and soul-expansion. Drake intimated that souls continued their growth here after physical death, fostering deeper understanding of love, relationships, and creativity. Vinnie found the prospect mesmerizing, imagining eons spent absorbing truth alongside equally curious beings.

But even as he basked in this transcendent realm, he felt echoes from Earth. He sensed that his body, now stabilized, lay in a hospital bed. He could feel sporadic prickles of pain, a distant reminder that his physical form was not yet out of danger. Then the presence of Drake enveloped him in a gentle hug, filling him with a surge of creative power so immense that he momentarily believed he could shape entire universes with a thought.

Suddenly, he heard the sound of prayer—a clear, imploring voice calling for Vinnie's recovery. It was his brother, standing by his hospital bed, commanding him, in the name of all that was holy, to be healed. The force of that prayer yanked him from the luminous domain. In a heartbeat, he was spiraling downward, losing sight of Drake and the remarkable spaces they had explored together. A jolt of pain shot through him as he blinked his eyes open, finding himself in a hospital ward, gasping for breath and blinking under the fluorescent glare.

The date was January 18th. Vinnie had been declared dead in a body bag and cut free just hours earlier. By January 21st, miraculously, he was released from the hospital—a rapid improvement that astonished the medical staff. They had expected weeks of rehabilitation or a vegetative state, if he survived at all. Instead, Vinnie walked out, albeit weak and shaken, but possessing his faculties and a heart brimming with spiritual insight.

Re-acclimating to earthly life proved an emotional gauntlet. Vinnie was beset by a deep longing for the love and harmony he had experienced on the Other Side. Where once he had been driven by building his physique or constructing homes, he now found himself searching for that intangible sense of unity and compassion. Drake's words rang in his mind: "It's going to be hard, but it's going to be worth it." He interpreted that as a reminder that living in the mortal world—with all its conflicts and misunderstandings—can seem daunting, yet it holds unique opportunities for growth and love.

In April of that same year, Vinnie's life took another unexpected turn when he met a woman named Andrea. Almost instantly, he recognized a spark that Drake had hinted would come. Their bond felt strangely familiar, as though they had known each other well before either's birth. Andrea's presence reawakened in Vinnie the desire to stay, to plant himself firmly on Earth and move forward. With her, he found a renewed sense of purpose, weaving lessons from his near-death experience into everyday acts of kindness, empathy, and honesty.

A few months later, Vinnie found himself attending a family reunion in Afton, Wyoming. Surrounded by cousins and uncles in a cozy mountain lodge, they huddled around old photographs tracing the family's lineage. A sepia-toned portrait drew Vinnie's attention: a strapping young man in simple attire. He nearly dropped the photo when recognition flared—those eyes, that facial structure. It was unmistakably the guide he had called "Drake." Enquiries revealed the man's real name was Charles, his great-grandfather, a figure unknown to him in life but evidently linked to him in spirit. The synchronicity left him breathless, reinforcing the authenticity of all he had witnessed in that luminous domain.

Since then, Vinnie openly shares what he has gleaned: that life on Earth is just a fraction of existence, and death—far from an ending—is more like a pivot point to a realm saturated with love and possibility. He emphasizes the lessons he gleaned from Drake: the value of being authentic, the necessity of learning to love and connect sincerely, and the abiding truth that material possessions pale compared to the relationships we foster. "We lived an eternity before this mortal life," Vinnie often says, "and we'll continue long after." He believes that the connections of the heart and the lessons we learn define our spiritual progression, not how many houses we build or how many trophies we earn in a bodybuilding competition.

He also encourages open-mindedness regarding "miracles," pointing out that if a rookie paramedic hadn't listened to his intuition that day, Vinnie's story would have ended zipped inside a body bag. His survival and subsequent exploration of the afterlife serve as a testament to how a single moment of compassion or faith can reroute someone's destiny.

Nowadays, Vinnie's life looks very different from his pre-2003 existence. He maintains a simpler outlook, focusing on family, forging sincere friendships, and nurturing spiritual growth. He still values health, but now not merely for aesthetic or competitive reasons, but as a means of honoring the sacredness of bodily life. Each day, he awakens to the memory of the radiant realm he glimpsed, recalling the boundless love that anchored him there. Whenever challenges arise—be they personal conflicts, stressors, or the physical aches that occasionally linger—he meditates on Drake's gentle instructions and the overwhelming love he felt in that other place.

Although Vinnie occasionally yearns for the warmth and acceptance of that higher dimension, the prospect of returning there one day no longer terrifies him but gives him comfort. He has a new lease on life, determined to spread messages of love, personal authenticity, and the importance of relationships over material gain. Drake's words, "It's going to be hard, but it's going to be worth it," echo as an ongoing mantra in his heart. And so, he continues forward—transformed, grateful, and hopeful— knowing that the best measure of a life isn't found in acco- lades, but in the unseen, heartfelt bonds that connect each soul to the next.

———

AFTERWORD

As you turn the final page of *The Other Side: Stories From the Afterlife*, you've journeyed through fourteen extraordinary narratives—each one a window into an experience that defies the boundaries of life as we know it. These are not just stories; they are testimonies of individuals who have glimpsed beyond the veil, touching something vast, mysterious, and deeply transformative. Whether encountering overwhelming love, breathtaking landscapes, or profound revelations, each person's account invites us to reconsider what we think we know about life, death, and what might lie beyond.

What is most striking across these diverse experiences is not their uniformity, but their profound personal resonance. Some describe radiant beings of light, others feel the presence of lost loved ones, and many speak of an overwhelming sense of peace—a peace that words can scarcely capture. And yet, despite the differences in detail, there is a shared thread: a deeper connection to something greater, an undeniable shift in perspective that often alters the course of the experiencer's life forever.

But these stories are not here to convince you of anything. They are not arguments for or against any particular belief system. Instead, they are offerings—intimate reflections of moments where the ordinary collided with the extraordinary. They ask not for acceptance, but for contemplation. They invite us to sit with the mystery, to ponder the possibilities, and perhaps to find comfort in the notion that death may not be an end, but a transition.

For some readers, these accounts may affirm what you've always felt to be true. For others, they might raise more questions than answers. That's the beauty of exploring the unknown: it stretches the mind and stirs the soul. And perhaps, that is the point—not to arrive at a final conclusion, but to remain open to wonder.

As we close this collection, may these voices linger with you, not as echoes from distant realms, but as reminders of the profound mystery woven into the fabric of our very existence. Life, it seems, is far more expansive than we can imagine—and death, perhaps, is just another chapter in an infinite story.

Thank you for walking this path with us, even if just for a while.

———

AFTERWORD

Want to experience more NDEs?
Visit our website and YouTube Channel

https://othersidende.com/
https://www.youtube.com/@TheOtherSideNDEYT